bluebird

bluebird

WOMEN AND

THE NEW PSYCHOLOGY

OF HAPPINESS

ariel gore

FARRAR, STRAUS AND GIROUX
NEW YORK

Farrar, Straus and Giroux
18 West 18th Street, New York 10011

Grateful acknowledgment is made for permission to reprint an excerpt from "Midrash on Happiness," by Grace Paley, from Long Walks and Intimate Talks *by Grace Paley and Vera B. Williams. Copyright © 1991 by Grace Paley. Used by permission of the Feminist Press at the City University of New York.*

Library of Congress Cataloging-in-Publication Data
Gore, Ariel, 1970–
    Bluebird : women and the new psychology of happiness / Ariel Gore — 1st ed.
    p. cm.
    Includes bibliographical references.
    ISBN 978-0-374-11489-3 (hardcover : alk. paper)
    1. Women.   2. Happiness.   I. Title.

HQ1155.G67 2010
305.42—dc22

2009015677

Designed by Abby Kagan

www.fsgbooks.com

1   3   5   7   9   10   8   6   4   2

The names of some of the individuals whose journal extracts are featured in this book have been changed.

Be strong. We have the right to make the universe we dream. No need to fear "science" groveling apology for things as they are, ALL POWER TO JOY, which will remake the world.

—DIANE DI PRIMA

contents

※

preface

❋

I must have been about nine years old when my paternal grand-mother gave me the gift of a small glass bluebird. "It's a symbol of happiness," she told me.

I turned it over in my hand. "Why?" I asked. I'd already learned that the color blue represented sadness.

My grandmother smiled at me, then frowned. "Ariel," she said gravely. "You ask too many questions. A nice young lady doesn't ask so many questions."

I put the glass bluebird in my hip pocket.

"Now smile and say 'Thank you,'" my grandmother instructed me.

I smiled and said "Thank you," but I kept on asking too many questions.

bluebird

introduction

When I was a twenty-year-old single mom and freshman in college, I signed up for a psychology and literature course because it was offered at the precise hour for which I'd found a babysitter. A small magical coincidence, it turned out, because there on the required reading list I came upon the dearest book—*A Life of One's Own* by the British psychotherapist Marion Milner. Originally published in 1934 under the pseudonym Joanna Field, the narrative follows Milner's seven-year "study of living" that began with a diary she started keeping when she was twenty-six years old. Her idea was that if she recorded the best moments in her daily life, she might begin to trace patterns from those moments and discover the conditions for lasting happiness. I marveled at the concept. *What an embarrassingly simple idea.*

I'd been traveling since I left home and school four years earlier. Because I was in almost-constant motion, the rhythm of a night train had become as familiar as my own heartbeat. I'd returned to California to start college only because the vagabond lifestyle proved tricky with a baby. I'd been running from depression and psychic death, searching and tripping in a mad-dash quest for . . . *what?* I wanted to prove to myself that I could survive without all the things the world told me I needed in order to survive, but I was seeking something, too. I hoped to find the antidote to depression, but I wouldn't have called it happiness at the time.

I mean, happiness was so uncool.

At best, happiness meant you were shallow and disconnected. More likely, it meant you were dumb. How could anyone be happy when the world was such a war-torn and miserable place? Happiness was hokey, optimism for dimwits. In my philosophy class I'd just written a paper arguing that human nature was basically mean-spirited. Still, I nursed my daughter to sleep and stayed up late California nights reading that little book called *A Life of One's Own*. It shocked my imagination that one woman's humble search for happiness might be an intellectual pursuit worthy of college-level inquiry. It reminded me of night trains and made me feel safe to see that an educated writer like Milner could admit that she, like me, didn't really know what she wanted. "Perhaps if one really knew when one was happy one would know the things that were necessary for one's life," she wrote.

Before I even finished the book, I started my own diary. I didn't write every day, but when I remembered and when I had time, I picked out the moments in which I'd been particularly happy and recorded them on lined pages.

Life isn't as simple as a series of inspirations and consequences, of course—all kinds of things influence us and bend our destinies—but I think it's fair to say that it was from those fragments and scribbles of experience that I found the thread that would embolden me to build the creative life and independent family I could nurture and be nurtured by as I stepped into adulthood.

Fast-forward fifteen years. I'm a full-time writer and the mother of a teenager. A cold spring afternoon and I'm stuck in traffic, listening to NPR, when an announcer notes: "At Harvard University this semester, students are flocking to a new class that might give them some insight into the secret to happiness. Psychology 1504—or Positive Psychology—has become the most popular course on campus."

I thought of my freshman year and smiled. Harvard had finally caught up with the little California hippie college where I'd spent my first two years as an undergrad. When I got home, I searched for the class on the Internet and downloaded the syllabus. I would read along with the Harvard kids, I decided. I had long since forgotten about *A Life of One's Own*, but in recent years I'd noticed a growing disconnect between the things I imagined would make me happy and the things that actually did. Potentially ego-boosting rites of passage in my career, for example—awards or good reviews—only seemed to cause me anxiety. Allowing myself to be absorbed in my work, on the other hand, whether it was writing or teaching or doing some familial chore I outwardly complained about, brought a quiet contentment I could feel radiate from my chest.

I'd always kept an irregular journal, but as I looked back through those pages now, I was embarrassed by the litany of complaints. In February, I was tired and stressed-out. In April, a friend had spited me. One night in June, I'd stayed up until dawn worrying about my daughter. And in August, I pretty much despised everyone I'd ever met. I'd recorded all the things that made me *un*happy, but what made me happy? Maybe a course in this new positive psychology was just what I needed. Maybe it would carry me back to that Marion Milner–inspired moment of insight and action. I started reading articles online, followed the latest studies, and devoured books on the science of joy. I read *Authentic Happiness*, *The Question of Happiness*, *The Happiness Hypothesis*, *Stumbling on Happiness*, "Some Dark Thoughts on

Happiness," and the *Journal of Happiness Studies*, and I checked out the World Database of Happiness.

Happiness, it turned out, had become serious business since I was a frosh. The field had ballooned since the late 1990s, when the psychologist Martin Seligman, author of *Learned Optimism* and then president of the American Psychological Association, convened a group of three leading male psychologists at a beach resort in Mexico. Intending to help shift the focus of modern psychology away from neurosis and pathology and toward resilience and well-being, they "invented" the new scientific movement.

Martin Seligman. That name rang a bell. I'd studied his work as an undergraduate, when I was getting my degree in communications. As a young psychologist, long before he launched this happiness craze, Seligman had become well-known for his work on the theory of learned helplessness. In a series of seminal experiments in the late 1960s, he and several other researchers administered electric shocks to groups of dogs. Some of the dogs could stop the shocks by pressing a lever. For other dogs, the shocks started and stopped at random intervals. The dogs who had some control over their experience quickly recovered from the ordeal, but the dogs who had no control soon began to exhibit symptoms similar to chronic depression.

The same dogs were later tested in a shuttle-box apparatus where they could escape the electric shocks by jumping over a low partition. The dogs who'd had control over the electric shocks in the first experiment quickly jumped out of their boxes. But most of the dogs who had previously learned that nothing they did mattered just covered their snouts with their paws and whined. They could have easily escaped the shocks, but they didn't even try. Essentially, they had learned to be helpless. In all the experiments, the strongest predictor of a depressive response was lack of control over negative stimulus.

This exercise in cruelty to animals opened a window into our understanding of the long-term consequences of abuse, oppression, and trauma.

And it was all these depressed dogs that eventually led Seligman to the beginnings of positive psychology. He started thinking about the few dogs that were the *exceptions* in these studies—the ones who seemed naturally resilient, who despite abuse never gave up their quest for freedom. *What was different about them?* He started thinking about the opposite of learned helplessness. If dogs—and people—could learn to be helpless, why couldn't they learn to be optimistic, too?

Twentieth-century psychotherapy and psychological study had focused on depression and illness—on getting folks from negative five to zero, as Seligman put it—but here was a new millennium, and Seligman and his buddies figured it was high time that scientists started looking at how to get us from zero to positive five. Because of his position and prestige, Seligman didn't have any trouble shoring up grant money and marketing his version of happiness studies for a broad audience.

Instead of spending more time cataloging the neuroses that cause our problems, Seligman and his colleagues would scientifically study the strengths and virtues that enable us to thrive. Instead of dissecting dysfunction, they would consider positive emotions, positive individual traits, and positive institutions. Instead of continuing to build on a science that supported only illness diagnoses, they would construct a new psychology that would support families and schools where kids could flourish, workplaces that would value worker satisfaction alongside productivity, and therapists who could identify and nurture patients' strengths.

Hallelujah, I thought.

But as I read deeper into the new literature, I started noticing something kind of *Twilight Zone* about this world of happiness studies. Everyone in this strange and smiley land, it seemed, was a guy. Take the Harvard professor Tal Ben-Shahar. Great guy. Sharp as a tack. In his book *The Question of Happiness*, each chapter opens with a quotation from another writer or philosopher. All twelve of them are men. Good men, for the most part—Aristotle and Gandhi as well as a few fellows I hadn't heard of—but all of them male. I started scrolling through authors and conference presenters and experts. Same story. It was like a Bohemian Club of academia. And then I noticed this: an intriguing number of the movement's critics were female. Barbara Held, for example, the author of *Stop Smiling, Start Kvetching*, owns the patent on the yellow smiley face with a slash through it. "First you feel bad," she says, "and then you're told you're defective for not being cheerful about it." A list of top positive psychology books on Amazon.com turned up example after example by men until I got to Julie Norem—and her book is called *The Positive Power of Negative Thinking*.

I was perplexed. *Didn't women want to be happy, too?* Still, I tried to ignore the imbalance. I didn't need to live in some feminist ghetto, after all, and I was glad to learn things from men. Not only had the positive psychology movement gained mainstream publishing success, but its basic tenets were starting to get taken seriously within traditional psychological and psychiatric institutions. Even the Gallup Organization, that great taker of surveys, had teamed up with positive psychologists and begun polling people around the world about their general sense of well-being.

As I read Martin Seligman's book *Authentic Happiness*, I looked forward to a chapter on parenting. I was already familiar with the conflicting data: When mothers are asked what brings them the most joy in life, they tend to respond without hesitation, "My kids." But when asked to keep a daily record of individual moments of joy, women report that they're actually happier reading, hanging out with friends, watching TV, or even doing the dishes than they are when interacting with their children. I could relate to both realities. Parenting, the source of daily heartbreaks and annoyances, has for me become a body of memory and experience that provides a sense of purpose that seems to cradle my general contentment. Surely Seligman's chapter on parenting would delve into this rich paradox. Imagine my disappointment when the chapter titled "Raising Children" focused entirely on using the principles of positive psychology to raise happy kids and not at all on the parent's experience of child-rearing. The omission seemed particularly strange because Seligman credits an exchange with his then-five-year-old daughter for inspiring the entire movement.

And Seligman's book wasn't the only one to leave me hanging.

As I delved into the growing body of research, I felt more and more left out. Most psychologists note that the emotional lives of men and women are different, but a majority of the commonly cited studies rely on male subjects. One exception: a famous study of nuns that looked at autobiographical essays written by a group of young sisters in the 1930s. Researchers found that the nuns who expressed faith and optimism in their essays lived longer than those who didn't. Seligman calls it "the most remarkable study of happiness and longevity ever done," but somehow it failed to capture my imagination. Grumpy nuns die young. So what? I couldn't help but start to wonder, *Are the complexities of women's lives outside the convent just too much for these happiness doctors to contemplate?*

Conventional wisdom holds that women are twice as likely as men to suffer a major depressive episode in their lifetimes.

Postpartum and maternal despair are so common that new motherhood is actually considered a major risk factor for depression. "In average emotional tone, women and men don't differ," Seligman notes, "but this strangely is because women are both happier and sadder than men." Here my interest was piqued. Now we were getting into something interesting. But Seligman leaves it at that. No further explanation or inquiry. Women are both happier and sadder than men. End of study.

Are we really both happier and sadder? Would there be any way to find out? Positive psychology has ignored women's issues, but women actually stand to benefit even more than men from psychological research that emphasizes strength, well-being, and resilience. If modern psychology has become overly focused on what's wrong with us, women have suffered more because of it. As the psychologist Phyllis Chesler noted in *Women and Madness,* "In my time, we were taught to view women as somehow naturally mentally ill. Women were hysterics (*hysteros,* the womb), malingerers, childlike, manipulative, either cold or smothering as mothers, and driven to excess by their hormones." When Chesler stood up at the 1970 American Psychological Association convention and demanded reparations "on behalf of women who had never been helped by the mental-health professions but who had, in fact, been further abused: punitively labeled, overly tranquilized, sexually seduced while in treatment, hospitalized against their wills, given shock therapy, lobotomized, and above all, unnecessarily described as too aggressive, promiscuous, depressed, ugly, old, angry, fat, or incurable," the mostly male audience laughed at her.

They *laughed.*

Since then, little has changed.

According to the World Health Organization, doctors are still more likely to diagnose depression in women even when our symptoms are identical to those of male patients. Being female is a significant predictor for being prescribed a psychiatric drug. And a major aim of all those drugs is to create artificial happiness. "No one ever taught me how to administer a test for mental health—only for mental illness," Chesler writes.

I was starting to feel kind of desperate when I found an Internet link to a study on "happy wives." Not all women are wives, of course, but at this point I wasn't going to be picky.

How exciting, I thought. *Click*.

But as I read the findings, my heart sank. Adding insult to exclusion, the 2006 study by the University of Virginia sociologists W. Bradford Wilcox and Steven Nock purported to show that married women with "traditional values" and breadwinning husbands were happier than married women with feminist values. My jaw dropped. I mean, were these boys serious? I could hardly wrap my increasingly unhappy feminist mind around what I read. Were these researchers actually trying to tell me that all I had to do to achieve lasting fulfillment was to embrace my inner hausfrau? Or, as Wilcox put it, "make an effort to expect less"?

I'm all for stay-at-home moms and traditional values if that lifestyle and those values reflect our true choices, but the implication here was that unless we're willing to compromise our core values and desires, we're doomed to a lifetime of misery. In a psychological field that had largely disregarded the female experience, I guess I shouldn't have been surprised—but I'd been trying to *learn optimism*.

In the American afterword to *A Life of One's Own*, Marion Milner cites a 1935 review of her book that concluded she'd been unhappy because she "had a job and a brain and that a woman's place is in the home and for a woman to exercise intelligence is to invite trouble." *How quaint*, I thought when I first read the passage. *So 1935.* But now the comment seemed some-how contemporary.

The "happy wives" study, which got more than its fair share of press with op-ed columns in *The New York Times* and the *Los Angeles Times* as well as mentions on network and cable TV, turned out to be highly questionable. Based on data from polls conducted in the early 1990s, the findings were so atypical as to render the whole study what's called an outlier. In fact, when the sociologist Scott Coltrane of the University of California at Riverside used the same data set, he found no difference in marital happiness between homemakers and women who worked outside the home. Still, the findings—or rather the publicity surrounding the findings—pointed up something important. Women's resistance to the happiness salesmen started to make more sense. When happiness is connected to certain behaviors like, say, scrubbing the kitchen floor without complaint, we smell an agenda. When joy is associated with selflessness and generosity, as it often is, we understandably recoil. We've already been overconditioned to be generous, to be selfless. Many of us compulsively give of ourselves at the expense of our own well-being. To advise a greedy, egocentric dude to do some charity work is one thing. To tell a mother, wife, and waitress who spends her days and nights in service to her family and community that generosity is the secret to happiness—and that if she's bummed out, it must be because she's not giving enough—is just absurd. Our tendency toward generosity isn't just an issue of gender, of course. We all know women who are selfish, and we all know men who would give us their last sweet potato, but gender is a huge factor in our conditioning.

It was with all this in mind that I began my own "study of living"—an adventure into the feminine history, science, and experience of happiness—intent on discovering the secret of joy.

I began keeping a journal again, and I recorded the happiest moments of each day. I interviewed hundreds of women via e-mail and in person, and then I convened a council of experts—artists, mothers, service workers, scholars, psychologists, and women's health-care providers. I invited the women of my council to keep their own journals for several weeks and then join me for a liberation psychology forum. I expected these women to share a few insights from their journals, but after a lively and emotional discussion most spontaneously handed me their personal writings. Their words—scrawled as they rode the bus to school or work, or in the quiet of the night after their children had gone to bed, or in a garden outside the hospital where they waited to get a mammogram—inform these pages. Their generosity is testament to our shared dream of the possibility of a new psychology, of a world in which women and all people who have been systematically taught that we don't deserve to be happy might finally jump out of our shock boxes and be free.

The vast majority of books on happiness include somewhere in their early pages a vague lament that we can't really *define* happiness. But if we want to learn to grow something, I think it's important to begin with some shared definition of what that thing is and what it isn't—even if that definition is necessarily seedlike. As I read all the research and interviewed women about their experience of happiness, it became clear that happiness isn't the absence of sadness. Happiness doesn't require us to suppress our other emotions or emotional states. Happiness often creeps up on us unexpectedly, but it can also be an act of will—a choice. We don't have to be happy. Sometimes we choose happiness.

The Canadian positive psychologist Paul T. P. Wong defines happiness simply as "the capacity to rejoice in the midst of suffering." I like that definition. Happiness isn't the absence of suffering. Happiness doesn't have to be about denial.

In his delightfully trippy little book, *The Hidden Messages in Water*, Masaru Emoto writes, "Your definition of happiness will depend upon who you are—but do you have a sense of peace in your heart, a feeling of security about your future, and a feeling of anticipation when you wake up in the morning? If we can call this happiness, then would you say that at this moment you are happy?"

So that's the open question we begin with. We're apt to find some surprising answers.

"As for the method which led me to these discoveries," Marion Milner warned readers in her 1934 introduction to *A Life of One's Own*, "let no one think it is an easy way because it is concerned with moments of happiness rather than with stern duty or high moral endeavor. For what is really easy, as I found, is to blind one's eyes to what one really likes, to drift into accepting one's wants ready-made from other people, and to evade the continual day-to-day sifting of values. And finally, let no one undertake such an experiment who is not prepared to find himself more a fool than he thought."

So let us push on, prepared to find ourselves fools.

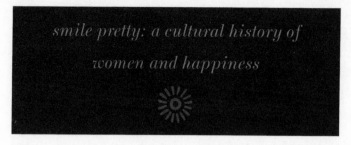

smile pretty: a cultural history of women and happiness

The young wife . . . owes it to her husband and to the world, to be cheerful. She is seldom aware of the amazing importance of this quality to her own happiness, as well as to that of others.

—WILLIAM ALCOTT, *The Young Wife*, 1837

the truth we are trying not to know

✳

*It made me happy to withdraw my job application and go to the café
instead, read and write and eat blackberry cobbler and watch the rain.*
—FROM ARIEL'S JOURNAL

New Year's Day arrives with freezing rain and news of closed
bridges. I decline dinner invitations, explain that I'm tired and
nauseous and "anyway, I'm not drinking right now." I'm surprised when these little clues don't give me away. "I'm six weeks
pregnant," I have to explain, rather slowly.

Friends and family react with wide eyes and stunned silences.

"Is this a joke?" my mother practically screams into the
phone.

It's not that I'm too young, as they thought I was when I got
pregnant with my daughter at eighteen. It's not even that they
think I'm too old. It's just that . . . *it's been so long.*

I have my own quiet doubts about my choice. I've always
wanted to have a second child, but the opportunity was slow to
present itself. By the time my daughter started high school, I figured I'd missed my chance. *Who has children more than fifteen years
apart?* As college catalogs arrived in the mail and Maia studied
for her SATs, I readied to change my life, too. I would be an
empty nester by the time I turned thirty-seven, finally able to do

all the things I'd heard women without children do—like work even harder. I applied for a job in a cold city. I could finally make some real money. My partner was about to open a community acupuncture clinic and didn't want to move, and I didn't want to sell my house in Portland, so I planned to commute the two thousand miles. I'd rent a studio apartment in the cold city, fly home on the weekends. When I envisioned my new life, it seemed hard and dark and serious. I saw myself trudging through arctic winds between concrete studio and concrete institution, but I didn't question the wisdom of my plan. It made good financial sense, after all, and who was I to question good financial sense?

When the desire to have another baby whispered in my ear, I tried to ignore it. I told myself that the quiet voice was fear in disguise—having a kid at home was the only way I'd ever known adult life. Surely all mothers of teenagers felt this strange urge to begin again. I decided to ask around. I posed the question to one friend and then another, but my mother-friends shook their heads and laughed. With teenage children on their way out the door, these moms had no longing to "go back." I wanted to feel the way they did, the way I understood I was supposed to feel—relieved, finished. And for a time, I convinced myself that I did. But then something inside of me started to shift.

Maybe the only thing harder than facing an honest desire is denying it.

I was out at a smoky underground tavern, Etta James on the jukebox, sharing a beer with a friend who'd always said she wanted to have a child. She talked as casually as she always had about finding the right partner, getting her career to a more stable place.

"You'll be forty next year," I finally blurted, almost spraying her with my beer. "You still think the perfect time and situation is just going to present itself? If you want to have a kid, you've got to work harder and smarter toward your goal."

She looked at me the way people look at you when you've just said something horribly inappropriate. And then she changed the subject.

A few days later, I sat in a folding chair in the shade of a sprawling California oak tree at the memorial service for my stepfather. He'd been the father I'd known, the one who helped build the playhouse in my kindergarten schoolyard, the one who showed me the beauty of a high Sierra mountain trail, the one I called from a pay phone on the coast of Spain when I realized I was pregnant with Maia. I scanned the row of faces to my left now—my mother and grandmother, my sister and nephew, my nearly grown daughter. It had been a long year of death in our extended family. My daughter's father had died unexpectedly in his early fifties, my partner's mother in her sixties, a young writer-friend in her early twenties, and now my rock of a stepdad in his late eighties. I closed my eyes. *Enough death already*, I thought. When I opened my eyes, I looked up into the branches of that old oak tree, and without running the idea past the good and practical critics in my brain, I said to God or to my stepdad or just to the tree and the blue sky behind it, "I'll have another one if you want me to."

When we got home to Portland, I told my partner that I was ready to have another kid. She was game. Maria had wanted a baby since we got together six years earlier—I'd been the ambivalent one. Now we made lists of sperm banks, open adoption agencies, and possible known donors. I started tracking my cycle. I'd take my own advice and work hard and smart toward my goal. We'd try everything at once and see which path opened up in front of us.

Three months later, I was pregnant.

Taking the job in that cold city and having a baby weren't mutually exclusive, exactly, but by the time those two pink lines showed up on the pregnancy test, it had become clear that I didn't want to go anywhere.

It's funny the way the right decision only seems obvious once you've made it.

When I read the beginning of Elizabeth Gilbert's book *Eat, Pray, Love,* I understood how she felt. At age thirty-one, despite a lifetime spent building toward that mythic moment when she'd get pregnant and "settle down" as she understood she was supposed to, it hit her like a revelation: "I was trying so hard not to know this, but the truth kept insisting itself to me." In the face of every "supposed to" she knew, she had to confront the reality that she didn't want to be married anymore, didn't want to live in her big house anymore, and didn't want to have a baby.

There are choices we can go either way with in this life. And then there are the truths that keep insisting themselves to us.

Gilbert's vision is a throwback to another writer born more than a century earlier. When Charlotte Perkins Gilman collapsed with depression in the 1880s, she sought the treatment of the renowned "nerve specialist" Dr. S. Weir Mitchell. She showed up in his Philadelphia office with the earnest hope for a cure, and told him everything she had observed about her case. Her sickness vanished when she was away from her husband and daughter, she explained, but returned as soon as she got home. The arrogant Dr. Mitchell wasn't interested in Gilman's own observations about her life. His prescription was simple: "Live as domestic a life as possible . . . Lie down an hour after each meal. Have but two hours intellectual life a day. And never touch pen, brush or pencil as long as you live."

Gilman managed to follow the good doctor's orders for a few years, but she sank deeper into her depression. "I would sit blankly moving my head from side to side," she later wrote. "I would crawl into remote closets and under beds . . . to hide from the grinding pressure of that distress."

In her 1892 short story, "The Yellow Wallpaper," she wrote, "If a physician of high standing, and one's own husband, assures friends and relatives that there is really nothing the matter with one but temporary nervous depression—a slight hysterical tendency—what is one to do?"

Finally, "in a moment of clear vision," Gilman woke up to the source of her illness. She divorced her husband and took off for California, baby in tow—and with pen, brush, and pencil all close at hand.

More than a hundred years later, how many of us can hear the truths that keep insisting themselves to us? How many of us can listen? How many of us can act on our moments of clear vision? Our desires have been patronized and pathologized for so long it takes serious courage to acknowledge that they even exist.

"I was surprised as I started keeping this happiness journal," said Sonja, a doctor in her mid-thirties and one of the women on my council of experts. "The question of contentment came up for me almost every day. I was content to be at work. I am happy enough. But am I content just to be content? I want to be happy.

My mom was sort of a malcontent until she found out that she was very ill and dying. Then she got content. She did a good job of it, but she wasn't happy. It was just good enough. I want more."

Britt, a student and waitress in her mid-twenties, chimed in: "We're made to feel selfish for making choices based on our own happiness instead of on other people or on our career. Sometimes I have to shake myself and say, 'I'm not selfish! This is *my* life!'"

It takes bravery to honor our right to make our own decisions; it takes work to uncover buried longings. It's a lot of trouble not to do what's expected of us. Every decade, the Dr. S. Weir Mitchells of the world—the talk show psychologists, advice columnists, and "experts"—come up with new formulas for what they say will make us happy. But do these new formulas work? Do they serve us?

"Have you any notion how many books are written about women in the course of a year?" Virginia Woolf asked an audience of women in 1929. "Have you any notion how many are written by men? Are you aware that you are, perhaps, the most discussed animal in the universe?"

It's no wonder we've gotten a little jaded.

In the introduction to *The Second Sex*, Simone de Beauvoir put the happiness argument into perspective, saying,

> Are not women of the harem more happy than women voters? Is not the housekeeper happier than the working-woman? It is not too clear what the word happy really means and still less what true values it may mask. There is no possibility of measuring the happiness of others, and it is always easy to describe as happy the situation in which one wishes to place them. In particular those who are condemned to stagnation are often pro-

nounced happy on the pretext that happiness consists in being at rest. This notion we reject.

"I am interested in the fortunes of the individual as defined not in terms of happiness but in terms of liberty," de Beauvoir concluded.

Fair enough, but I propose that we can now interest ourselves in the fortunes of the individual when it comes to both our happiness and our liberty.

We can insist on liberty because we know it's the foundation for long-term happiness. We know that our immediate experience might be easier if we bit our tongues and did what was expected of us—if we allowed ourselves to be condemned to stagnation—but we reject the notion that happiness consists in being at rest. Stagnant happiness isn't the happiness we're looking for.

We are here to evolve.

In *Eat, Pray, Love*, Gilbert describes running into an acquaintance who'd just found out she was pregnant. The woman was ecstatic, had always wanted to be a mother. "I saw the joy in her face and I recognized it," Gilbert writes. "This was the exact joy my face had radiated last spring, the day I discovered that the magazine I worked for was going to send me on assignment to New Zealand, to write an article about the search for giant squid. And I thought, 'Until I can feel as ecstatic about having a baby as I felt about going to New Zealand to search for a giant squid, I cannot have a baby.'"

Our bodies and our imaginations and our sleep patterns rebel when we try to trick ourselves into lives we don't really want. Still, there are plenty of doctors, psychologists, acquaintances, and relatives who are more than eager to help us deny our truths and do what's expected of us—to stay with the husband and have the baby, to take the fancy job in the cold city, to never touch pen, brush, or pencil as long as we live. We are told what will make us happy as if we were all the same woman, as if we all share a single heart, as if we can't all be right when we realize our disparate desires: another child, an intellectual life, more than contentment, a giant squid.

creating reality

※

I've been obsessively thinking about happiness. I've been disturbed that my happiness seems to be based on external forces rather than an internal sense of joy that permeates my life. This has brought me to the question: How do I reach that underlying current of joy?
—FROM ROSLYN'S JOURNAL

A child of the 1970s in California, I was constantly told, "You create your own reality." But I lived in a house I did not design, breathed air I did not pollute, went to public schools I did not vote to underfund, rushed home as soon as the last bell rang to avoid the flasher who skulked in the yard across the street, ate off beautiful antique dishes I neither made nor worked for, and slept soundly between soft sheets.

I did not create my own reality.

"Ah, but that's because you hadn't yet taken responsibility for your own life," the New Agers would insist, sipping their bee pollen tonics and adjusting their crystal pendants.

Back then, as now, I understood their point: *that which we water grows.* But I also understood that most of them were privileged and narcissistic.

You create your own reality, they said. It's an idea that can be potent and empowering: if I can dream it, I can make it happen.

But the belief has a dark side, too. Cancer patients are made to feel that they brought their illness upon themselves because of their own negative thinking. Underemployed workers are sent to career counseling, where they're taught that their real problem is their own sorry view of themselves. And I guess that folks living and dying through wars can assume that they're just not good enough at visualizing world peace.

I'm all for magical thinking, but I'm wary of its pushers. When 1 percent of the population controls some 96 percent of our resources, it's probably in their best interest to convince the rest of us to close our eyes, relax, and trust the universe. If we're all busy mumbling, "I am wealthy, empowered, and happy," focusing entirely on affirmation and not at all on action, we are less likely to rise up and make it so.

Is one person's long-term unemployment the result of her own poor self-image? Or is her poor self-image the result of long-term unemployment? Perhaps both are the consequence of an educational and economic system that stacks the deck against some and in favor of others.

We've all met people who seem to suffer from victim complexes—people who unnecessarily perpetuate their own problems, who shoot themselves in the foot and beg us to do the same—but most people's wounds are not self-inflicted.

Just yesterday I saw a beautiful, ruddy-faced little boy all dressed up like a pirate. He was maybe four or five years old. He wore his red bandanna and black eye patch proudly as he marched to see the tall ships on display in a small-town port. When he caught his first glimpse of those fancy ships, I guess he got a little overexcited, because he moved to dash for the pier. A woman who looked to be his grandmother grabbed the back of his white T-shirt to stop him, but it wasn't a hey-wait-and-be-safe kind of grab; it was an angry grab. I know as well as anyone that young children can be trying, so I didn't think much of the grandmother's bad mood. The boy whined, his pirate bandanna and eye patch a little askew. He held tight to the plastic toy sword at his side as he struggled to break free from the fist that held him. And then, sudden as a shift in the wind, the bad mood of the scene turned ugly. A cold kind of hatred fixed itself on the grandmother's face. Without warning, she let go of the boy's shirt so that he fell, flat on his face, onto the cement, without a moment's chance to protect himself. He wailed a brokenhearted, broken-boned kind of wail. The grandmother just stood there, a stone statue of rage, no visible remorse or instinct to help the boy. "That's what you get fer pullin'," she seethed, as if he'd brought the abuse on himself—as if he'd created his own bruised- or broken-nosed reality.

If we are to believe that we all create our own realities, we'd have to say that the grandmother was right: *That's what you get fer pullin'*. We'd have to take a look at the hierarchy of the world and assume, too, that white people are better visualizers than people of color, and that men are more astute when it comes to manifesting their dream jobs than women.

This is a book about shaping our own realities—about better understanding our emotional lives so we might become more active players in their creation—so I think it's important to consider in what ways we create our realities. Because, as it turns out, women's notions about personal happiness are all tangled up with our ideas about privilege, selfishness, and social responsibility.

When I interviewed women about their thoughts and experiences of happiness, I was surprised by how many expressed an inner conflict. The women had no trouble talking about their fondest memories or what they believed might make them happier, but at some point in the conversation they voiced a basic question: "How can we be happy when so many people on earth are living in horrible situations?" This held true for women of virtually every class and education level.

As one woman put it, "I will be happy when no one in the world suffers." Maybe this is just a cop-out—a noble excuse not to figure out what would make us happy—but it points to some basic beliefs many of us share.

"Happiness seems almost distasteful when you think about all the sadness out there," another woman said.

In his book *Happier*, the Harvard professor Tal Ben-Shahar emphasizes the importance of a change in values and focus. He encourages us to teach ourselves to see happiness, not money or power, as "the ultimate currency." But when I asked my council of experts what they would do differently if they saw happiness as their primary goal—as the ultimate currency—Jennifer, an artist with a day job in her mid-forties, summed up the way a lot of women feel: "I think I might already behave as though happiness is the ultimate currency. My mother calls it 'only doing what you want to do,' or selfishness, or childishness."

I shouldn't have been surprised that this notion of selfishness would come up so soon. As women, we have been taught that thinking of ourselves is intrinsically selfish.

In Carol Gilligan's revolutionary book on psychological theory and women's development, *In a Different Voice*, she lays out findings that female morality and decision-making tend to focus on our sense of responsibility and care, while the male approach tends to be justice-oriented. She explains the sometimes-subtle difference this way: "While an ethic of justice proceeds from the premise of equality—that everyone should be treated the same—an ethic of care rests on the premise of nonviolence—that no one should be hurt."

When it comes to feminine moral development, Gilligan breaks it down into three basic stages. As girl children in the first stage of our moral development, we're all pretty selfish. "Me" and "mine" all the way. As we're taught to care for others, and taught that selfishness is wrong, we move into a second stage—a "conventional stage" of morality. Now we feel it's wrong to act in our own interests, and we learn to worry about everyone else. In the conventional stage, we come to understand that concern for ourselves makes us selfish. A lot of us get stuck at this conventional stage. But there's a third stage—a "post-conventional stage" of development. Now we begin to understand that it's just as wrong to ignore our own needs as it is to ignore the needs of others. Connection and relationship involve more than one of us, after all, and if anyone is slighted—ourselves included—the relationship is harmed and something immoral has taken place.

"When nations are wealthy and not in civil turmoil and not at war," Martin Seligman told *The Boston Globe* in the spring of 2006, "they start asking what makes life worth living, and that's what positive psychology is about." But that seriously limits the scope of the smiley science, doesn't it? What brings us meaning when we're struggling is at least as important as what makes it all worthwhile when we're successful. If we limit our inquiry to people who have privilege, who have maximum control over their lives in the form of money, security, and good health, why not also actively exclude people who don't—say, single parents, people with disabilities, or the entire working class? Why not exclude women?

As far as I'm concerned, a psychology that doesn't consider huge chunks of the population is no psychology at all. As anyone who's ever run out of grocery money before the end of the month can tell you, the pursuit of happiness is hardly just a rich kids' adventure. We want groceries, but we want to feel confident and fulfilled as well.

The Canadian psychologist Paul T. P. Wong challenges all researchers to move beyond "the comfortable confines of American positive psychology which focuses on personal happiness and individual success in 'normal people' under normal or benign conditions." He advocates what he calls a "radical" or "mature" positive psychology that focuses on contentment, humility, meaning, and acceptance—even in the midst of suffering.

One woman I interviewed, a mother who had a toddler with a rare leukemia-like disease who nevertheless considered herself "quite happy," noted that "life sucks for a lot of people on earth. The whole you-make-your-own-happiness ideal is a little sick when you consider that."

Even among healthy people in nations that "are wealthy and not in civil turmoil and not at war," the notion that we create our own realities can get seriously oversimplified.

When I was in graduate school and getting by on about eight hundred dollars a month, a good friend inherited a large chunk of money. Within a few months, she started talking about "abundance theory" and "manifesting prosperity." She lectured me about my "poverty mentality" and lent me books to help me adjust my attitude and open myself to the universal affluence God meant for me to live in. "You create your own reality," she told me, earnest as could be.

The fact that her reality was created, at least in part, by a wealthy father who died young seemed lost on her.

My friend was incredibly proud of me a year later when I finished grad school and sold my first book. "See," she insisted. "The visualizations worked."

She was right—partly. I *had* been visualizing abundance. I'd read her books and meditated on attracting some cash, but I'd also worked diligently. I'd deferred the chance to make more money while I finished school, I'd played by the rules of capitalism in the publishing world, I'd used the privilege I already had and acted as though I deserved more, and I'd gotten lucky. I'd taken an active role in the creation of my reality, but I hadn't manifested that book deal with positive thinking alone.

The search for happiness is a spiritual quest, but it's a material quest, too. We want to find meaning and joy in this life on this earth. We can see that the prize we're after might be considered selfish, but it isn't a selfish happiness we want.

Happy people do not colonize land that already belongs to other people. They do not drop bombs, exploding lives and earth. Happy people do not lie to our face, stab us in the back, then scamper home muttering self-righteous justifications. And happy people do not drop their grandchildren face-first on the ground.

The educator A. S. Neill wrote, "All crimes, all hatreds, all wars can be reduced to unhappiness."

Happiness may be uncool, but our refusal to be happy doesn't make us more compassionate—it makes us mean.

Remember Paul T. P. Wong's simple definition of happiness: "the capacity to rejoice in the midst of suffering."

"Keeping this journal coincided with a very difficult time in my family," said Eleanor, a psychologist in her mid-thirties on my council of experts. "The timing was good because it really made me slow down at the end of each day and see that there were things that made me happy even in these difficult times. I realized that we can all have happiness, despite our struggles."

Consuelo, a nurse in her early sixties, put it this way, "The more I stayed in the present moment and refused to get caught up in a coworker being racist, sexist, or classist toward me, the more I could find happiness. A latte at three o'clock. That was happiness."

When Roslyn, a women's studies instructor in her mid-forties, got irritated with keeping the journal because she discovered that most of her happiness seemed to come from external events, she started meditating on the whole concept of joy. "That was my answer to the feeling that I lacked an intrinsic sense of happiness," she said. "Then I had a day when I was happy all day. It was a result of my meditation and also a result of paying attention. I called it forth."

We create our own reality thusly.

Without denial or narcissism, we muster the courage to face the world as it is, and we begin to take an active role in its transformation. We muster the courage to face our own lives just as they are and, even in the midst of suffering, rejoice.

THE FIRST QUESTION
How heavily do you weigh your own happiness
when making life decisions?

I asked a hundred women how much weight they gave their own happiness when making life decisions. Fewer than twenty-five said that happiness was, in fact, their primary consideration. Women with children often put their children's happiness before their own, and women with husbands or partners often noted that they consider their partner's happiness before their own. "There's a hierarchy of happiness," one woman explained to me. "First come the kids, then my husband, and then me. I'm stronger than they are. I don't need to be happy."

My own happiness is all I consider—as long as I'm not really hurting anybody.

Hugely. I was diagnosed with depression at age thirteen and know well by now that if I make decisions that impair my well-being, I will sink my battleship.

I grew up with a father who was prone to depression, and it tore the family apart when he was depressed. His unhappiness taught me to take care of myself first. I figure the best gift I can give my children is my own

*happiness. Obviously, the health and happiness of my husband and chil-
dren come into any decision-making prospect, but I won't make a decision that will surely make me unhappy—it's too much of a burden to
give everyone else.*

*My daughter comes first. My art comes second. These two make me
happy. Simple. Sometimes I have had to put off the latter to meet immediate needs of the former. As the sole supporter of my daughter, and being
such a young mother, I did have to at times compromise my art and happiness in order to survive, but being in college made a big difference. College gave me a community, an outlet for my expression and intelligence,
and a way to support my daughter.*

*Now that I'm single, I tend to factor my own happiness right after my
children's. New and different for me.*

*Until recently, most of my life decisions were made for what I perceived
to be my children's happiness. As a result, I am not very happy. And my
children certainly aren't thanking me for my sacrifice.*

*I'm very career-focused, so most of my decisions are about work and
work opportunities. I have long-term goals that will make me happy, but
in the meantime there is naturally a lot of sacrifice and long hours.*

*Making my husband and other people in my life happy makes me
happy.*

*It's weighing heavier now than it used to. I used to struggle more to do
what was "right"—as defined more by societal expectations, and expectations of those close to me. Now my happiness—or my life comfort—
is probably about a 50 percent factor.*

Generally, I can be pretty self-centered. I don't have kids, so that makes things a lot easier. But it's hard for me to be happy about a decision that would make other people unhappy. I also worry about the forces of capitalism influencing my decisions, especially in terms of material needs and wants.

I'm not sure what I consider. I often just jump in—to home-buying, marriage, getting knocked up. I don't stop to think about money or health or happiness.

I think I put most everyone else's happiness before my own.

Not at all.

a pretty girl is a girl with a smile on her face

※

*Okay, this is my second attempt today to write in this freaking jour-
nal. I thought about doing it a few times, but geez! It's 11:40 p.m.
and I just finished cleaning the kitchen.*
—FROM BRITT'S JOURNAL

I began to learn what it meant to be a woman in my paternal
grandparents' little yellow house on the Carmel beach, an idyllic
spot where my older sister and I were dumped for two-week
visits every summer and winter of our childhoods.

My mother's only instructions as we climbed out of our
wood-paneled station wagon and onto my grandparents' arched
driveway: "Don't forget to order the most expensive thing on
the menu."

We wore too-small jeans with holes in the knees and moth-
eaten sweaters so our grandmother would take us shopping.

My grandmother, for her part, hated my mother for reasons
innumerable and considered her, among other things, savagely
feminist. "In my day," my grandmother explained to me, "a
woman did not leave her husband. She took care of him." My
grandmother shook her head as she ran her fingers through her
short gray hair. "Now look at you girls. Children of divorce. It's
just so irresponsible."

After quick hugs and my grandmother's once-over, my sister and I climbed into the back of the gold Jaguar that never had crumbs in the seat, and we headed for the department store, where my grandmother bought us pink polo shirts and beige corduroy skirts.

Back in the little yellow house on the beach, dressed appropriately now as nice young ladies, my sister settled onto the couch with an Agatha Christie mystery, and I was schooled by my grandmother in the womanly arts of housekeeping, food service, and emotional management. *Someone has to do it*, she probably figured, and I was a willing student. My grandmother's ways seemed complicated and exotic to me, and her stiff emotional distance intrigued me. In her sensible tweed slacks and big round glasses, my grandmother looked, to my eyes, like the queen of England on a day off. "Now, Ariel," she would say, and then show me how to make the beds in each room with crisp hospital corners. She taught me to prepare lunch sandwiches assembly-line style: We'd lay out a dozen slices of white bread, then apply mayonnaise, mustard, romaine lettuce, American cheese, and sliced ham. We cut the sandwiches diagonally and set them in cloth-lined baskets, each with a small yellow bag of Lay's potato chips.

By lunchtime, the coastal fog had usually cleared, and my grandfather had made it home from his morning round of golf. We took the sandwich baskets outside to the glass table on the patio and served my grandfather first.

"Tell me what you bought today," my grandfather would ask, tapping his wooden leg. It made a soft, hollow sound with each thump.

In the evening, when the gray-blue ocean swallowed the sun, my grandmother and I set the dining room table while my grandfather watched the news and sipped his five o'clock cocktail. Spoons and knives on the right, forks on the left. "Now, Ariel," my grandmother explained, "you'll always remember this because 'spoon,' 'knife,' and 'right' all have five letters, while 'fork' and 'left' have only four letters. Spoon, knife, right; fork, left. Understand?"

I understood.

Before my grandmother served the plates of roast meat and potatoes, I circled the table like a waitress, taking orders. "Would you like green beans with your meat and potatoes, Grandpa? And will you take milk or gin?"

"Always smile, dear," my grandfather warned me. "A pretty girl is a girl with a smile on her face." He looked at my grandmother, and she parted her lips into a grin. She had a slight gap between her two front teeth. "A smile always makes everyone feel at ease," he said.

As women, I learned in Carmel, we were supposed to concern ourselves with whether or not everyone felt at ease. As women, we were to be not necessarily happy but pleasant.

My grandmother could smile on cue, smile to make other people happy, but I never saw my grandmother smile to herself. I watched her in the mornings sometimes, when she thought she was alone. As she gazed out the window at the sand dunes and the cypress trees, she always looked heartbroken.

She had a magnet on her refrigerator that said, "A woman can never be too rich, too thin, or have too many silk blouses." She was rich and thin and had a closetful of silk blouses. All her life, my grandmother had done as she was told. She married well and raised three kids, ended up with a beautiful piece of California beachfront property. But life had showered her with tragedy, too. Years of fear and confusion about her eldest son's puzzling behavior culminated when he was diagnosed with schizophrenia. As if this news weren't crushing enough, the prevailing medical theories of the time placed the blame squarely on Mom. She was the "schizophrenogenic" mother, they said, cold and unloving. She was the woman whose poor parenting had actually caused her son's disease. It didn't occur to early-twentieth-century psychiatrists that the detachment they observed in the mothers of some patients might be the *result* of raising kids with mental illnesses rather than the source of the problem. The theory of the schizophrenogenic mother has lost all credibility in the last thirty years, but from the 1940s and 1950s, when my grandmother was raising her kids, right up into the 1970s, when I came to know her as a sad and wealthy old woman who still wanted to do everything right, mental-health practitioners maintained that schizophrenia was single-handedly caused by mothers. This laid a pretty heavy burden squarely at a woman's feet for failing to exhibit the right emotions at precisely the right times.

A few years ago, I Googled the term "schizophrenogenic father" to see if anyone had written theories about my grandfather's behavior. He was at least as emotionally detached as my grandmother. No luck. Listing not a single reference, Google asked, "Did you mean: 'schizophrenogenic mother'?"

Sigh.

When I wasn't visiting my schizophrenogenic grandparents on the Carmel beach, I lived in a San Francisco suburb with my mother and stepdad, low-income intellectuals who never told anyone to smile. I think my mother considered it a sin of dishonesty to let any negative emotion go unexpressed. In high school, I ran with grumpy Goths until we all dropped out. I traveled the world then, sharing youth-hostel bunk beds with starry-eyed seekers and morose anarchists. In my twenties, I went to college and graduate school and hung out with pissed-off young feminists. We listened to Ani DiFranco sing, "If you're not angry, you're just stupid," and she was right and we were smart. So I was totally ill-prepared when, a few years later, my preteen daughter announced that she planned to try out for the middle-school cheerleading team. "I know you might not support my decision," she began. "And I can pay for my own uniform."

I assumed that my daughter's interest in this leading of cheers would be short-lived. I secretly wondered how she could possibly make the team. She, like me, had been accused of being less than friendly. Folks interpreted our lack of bubbly effervescence as arrogance—or depression. We were, it seemed to me, the last introverts in a vast nation of extroverts. But my daughter's interest was not short-lived. With a wild idea she worried her mother wouldn't approve of, she began a six-year odyssey in which she would not only be trained in the great American tradition of cheerfulness but actually be transformed into a leader of exhilaration, able to cajole the mood of an entire crowd.

As I started going to games and watching practices, I was fascinated. The girls entertained, they inspired enthusiasm, occasionally they taunted the competition, and they smiled—a lot. *What was it all about?*

Our European relatives nodded in bewildered recognition when I told them about Maia's new pastime. "Ah, yes," they said. "This is how they do it in America."

I noticed a few female football players over the years, and there were a couple of male cheerleaders on Maia's junior varsity team, but for the most part those being cheered as they grunted and ran were young men, and those doing the jumps and flips and cheering were young women.

This is, indeed, how we do it—as women and as Americans.

"As a matter of tradition, emotion management has been

better understood and more often used by women," Arlie Russell Hochschild tells us in *The Managed Heart: Commercialization of Human Feeling*. "Especially among dependent women of the middle and upper classes, women have the job (or think they ought to) of creating the emotional tone of social encounters: expressing joy at the Christmas presents others open, creating the sense of surprise at birthdays, or displaying alarm at the mouse in the kitchen." Hochschild doesn't think it's anything innate in female biology or psychology that makes us cheerleaders. She sees it as a habit we developed because we have, historically, depended on men for money, and we've learned that one of the ways we can repay our debt is by doing extra emotional work, "especially emotional work that affirms, enhances, and celebrates the well-being and status of others."

I raised my daughter primarily as a single mom. My own mother and stepdad didn't adhere to all the traditional gender roles in their marriage. My stepdad did most of the cooking, for example, and my mother was the one who could express anger. But tradition dies hard. Our grandparents' and great-grandparents' blood flows through our veins, too. I've rarely depended on men for money, and I've never consciously felt indebted to anyone, but I often notice that I choose old-school female deference and "niceness" when it comes to my behavior in relationships. It starts out as the authentic desire to share the love on a beautiful day, or to soothe ruffled feathers when things get rough, but when I'm pushed toward conflict, something inside of me shifts. I have an almost childish phobia of confrontation. I don't want people to be mad at me. I don't want to be accused of trying to dominate anyone with rage or force. Before I know it, my authentic emotional offering has morphed into full-on passive aggression. If I'm the better player at this emotional game—and usually I am—I'll get what I want without raising my voice, and my adversary will end up feeling like a jerk for not offering it to me in the first place. When I can see myself doing it, the habit seems almost laughable, but it's gotten me into some serious trouble. "You're living like an old woman in the south of Italy who has no possibilities," a friend once told me. I was nineteen years old and refusing to leave a boyfriend who ended arguments with his fist. "Not like an intelligent American woman who has been all over the world."

A generation of nontraditional gender talk and the fact that I didn't need my boyfriend in order to survive hadn't changed my basic belief that love, and my earnest emotional work, would have the power to change everything. *Maybe my boyfriend was violent because he didn't feel good about himself. Surely I could make him feel better. Perhaps if I could just be more pleasant—if I could make him feel at ease—things would be all right.*

"Always smile, dear," my grandfather had warned me for so many years. "A smile always makes everyone feel at ease."

"Smile!" my daughter's cheerleading coach cried out at practices even as the girls prepared to do their most dangerous stunts. "Always smile."

From culture and television, grandparents and coaches, we've learned that our role is to affirm, enhance, and celebrate the well-being and status of pretty much everyone but ourselves.

Go, Warriors!

Contemporary cheerleading culture is totally girl-dominated. From their short flippy skirts to the emotional work they do, cheerleading seems designed for women. And these days, some 97 percent of cheerleaders are female. But now let's throw a monkey wrench into our research: Gender doesn't explain everything. Cheerleading, it turns out, was once an all-male activity. We can trace cheerleading history to crowd chants and organized yelling back at Princeton and the University of Minnesota in the 1880s and 1890s. And the first cheerleader? One Johnny Campbell, a Minnesota undergraduate who stood in front of the crowd at an 1898 football game and led the fans in a spirited chant: "Rah, rah, rah! Sku-u-mar, hoo-rah! Hoo-rah! Varsity! Varsity! Varsity, Minn-e-so-tah!"

Even former president George W. Bush was once a cheer-leader.

Even more than being stereotypically female, all this cheering is *American.*

Maybe it's time to get out our history books.

welcome to the nation of can-do optimists

❋

I slept so well in M.'s arms. The sun is shining, the weather is sweet.
All I dream, all I see and feel, is beauty that surrounds me, beauty
that shines within me.

—FROM CALLIOPE'S JOURNAL

When I traveled through Asia and Europe as a teenager, I had a hard time convincing the people I met that I was American. Locals and fellow travelers took me for Canadian, Middle Eastern, southern European. They took me for Mexican, South American, Russian. They took me for anything but what I am: U.S. North American—at least three generations on each side.

"You're too quiet to be an American," they told me. "You're not friendly enough," they insisted. "Americans are such a cheery lot."

And on the whole, we are. Historians of emotion actually note a major shift in the American mood that took place more than two hundred years ago as the whole culture went from melancholy to merry.

Back in colonial days, sadness was cool. *Very Euro.* Tears signified a noble character. A long face showed that you were sensible and compassionate. British and American diarists alike portrayed themselves as mournful souls—men grieving and women crying. Christians understood suffering as a path to virtue. Puritans asked God to help them stay humble. From New England to Georgia, good Americans wept.

But then something funny happened. Folks hardly noticed it at first, but within a generation everything had changed. Only in hindsight was it obvious: with American independence, sadness started to fall out of fashion. Pessimism was for the weak. The Revolutionary War might have been rather unpleasant for the people fighting it, but the winners walked with a new spring in their step. Good cheer became a marker of self-sufficiency. *Who needs England, anyway?*

Thomas Jefferson wrote "the pursuit of happiness" into the Declaration of Independence as an inalienable right. He explained to his daughter Patsy that it was part of the American character "to consider nothing as desperate; to surmount every difficulty by resolution and contrivance, to find means within ourselves and not to lean on others." A smile meant that you were surmounting hard times like the good, strong kid you were. If you were bummed out, maybe you were just a needy good-for-nothing.

Women's rights advocates and early abolitionists were told to be patient when it came to their own inalienable rights, but the whole population became notably perky. European visitors commented on "the good humour of Americans." Bizarrely, even child factory workers were described as "cheerful and healthy." Self-determination may not have been a part of these kids' American experience, but they were told that with hard work and perseverance it might become their American reality. It was all about pursuit. *Chin up!*

The "American Dream" promised every broke orphan selling flowers on the street corner a shot at the big time. *A classless society! Step right up and become upwardly mobile!* The saying "You create your own reality" was unheard of, but we can see its roots clearly in all these early American notions about success and independence. Business failures were explained away by lack of moral and emotional control. As early as 1793, when a Philadelphia epidemic of yellow fever killed more poor people than affluent, a lot of folks concluded that the disease tended to strike "weak minds." I guess they didn't notice that most of the rich kids in Philly fled—and even those who stayed behind had better access to clean water.

With the rise of the American middle class came even more good cheer. Part of the class identity, after all, was based on learning to manage our emotions. The modern middle-class mind-set called for keeping our spirits up even in the face of adversity. Displays of happiness came to be seen as status symbols—a sign of prosperity even when there was no prosperity to speak of. In her paper "From Good Cheer to 'Drive-By Smiling': A Social History of Cheerfulness," the communication theorist Christina Kotchemidova writes that "the symbolic value of good cheer rose as it became a necessary part of attaining status in capitalism." Taking it further, she writes, "Moderns developed an impatience with helplessness, which was accompanied by a distaste for grief and later translated into male aversion to tears."

In 1837, the journalist Francis Joseph Grund noted that the average American seldom complained because "the sympathy he might create in his friends would rather injure than benefit him." In a nation built on the assumption that everyone ought to pursue happiness, failure to achieve that happiness meant you were a loser. Cheerfulness abounded, and "no one dared to show himself an exception to the rule."

As Americans' worldwide reputation for friendliness took hold, we ladies became responsible for a particular brand of happiness on demand.

A woman "owes it to her husband and to the world, to be cheerful," William Alcott told us in his 1837 book *The Young Wife*.

Women authors agreed. If you studied the art of housekeeping in 1869, you might have learned it from Catharine Beecher and Harriet Beecher Stowe's classic, *The American Woman's Home*:

> There is nothing which has a more abiding influence on the happiness of a family than the preservation of equable and cheerful temper and tones in the housekeeper. A woman who is habitually gentle, sympathizing, forbearing, and cheerful, carries an atmosphere about her which imparts a soothing and sustaining influence, and renders it easier for all to do right, under her administration, than in any other situation.
>
> The writer has known families where the mother's presence seemed the sunshine of the circle around her; imparting a cheering and vivifying power, scarcely realized till it was withdrawn. Every one, without thinking of it, or knowing why it was so, experienced a peaceful and invigorating influence as soon as he entered the sphere illumined by her smile, and sustained by her cheering kindness and sympathy. On the contrary, many a good housekeeper, (good in every respect but this), by wearing a countenance of anxiety and dissatisfaction, and by indulging in the frequent use of sharp and reprehensive tones, more than destroys all the comfort which otherwise would result from her system, neatness, and economy.

Who wouldn't want to be "the sunshine of the circle around her"? But what might that mean, to *more than destroy all the com-*

fort? Our failure to be that smiling sunshine didn't just mean we were bad housekeepers—it was worse than that.

The Victorian days brought not only the rise of the "expert" and all these advice books but also a strange epidemic of "nervous disorders" among women. Diaries from the time give us hundreds of examples of women falling into what would now be diagnosed as chronic fatigue or depression. Doctors called it "neurasthenia" or "Americanitis," "nervous prostration," "hyperesthesia," "melancholia," or the infamous "hysteria."

Good old Hippocrates, the Greek "father of medicine," coined that term—"hysteria"—and it was used to describe pretty much anything that ailed a woman's heart or mind. It included symptoms like anxiety, weakness, headaches, cold legs, muscle aches, water retention, menstrual problems, indigestion, grumpiness, troublemaking, and, my favorite, gnashing of teeth.

What caused this strange medical-emotional condition?

The uterus, of course.

Seeing it as the dominant organ in a woman's body, experts claimed that if we let that little womb of ours get "discontented and angry," it might just start wandering around our body in search of children. *The cure?* Hippocrates suggested marriage. By the late nineteenth century, the diagnosis had become as common as corsets. The preferred cure of the era was pelvic massage and "hysterical paroxysm"—otherwise known as orgasm. The diagnosis and treatment of women became big business. Dr. S. Weir Mitchell, the so-called greatest nerve specialist in the country, earned more than sixty thousand dollars a year (the equivalent of well over a million in today's economy), but, alas, some of those Victorian "nerve specialists" didn't enjoy the tedious task of massaging their patients to climax. And so it was, in the 1870s, perhaps the only good to come of all these bizarre and long-held medical theories, the invention of the vibrator. A great time-saving device for doctors, the first known electro-mechanical vibrator was used at a French asylum in 1873—for the treatment of hysteria.

Ah, to be a woman at any moment in Western history.

At the turn of the twentieth century, when the advertising industry as we know it really started taking shape, there was a curious shift in marketing strategy from the "warning" ad that convinced us, for example, to buy mouthwash because bad breath might lead to lifelong spinsterhood, to the "product satisfaction" ad that promised leisure and happiness if we just purchased this one particular mouthwash or insurance plan.

Advertisers learned to accentuate the positive, and the idea that success bloomed from optimism kept growing strong. Despite its European imagery, *The Secret*, the 2006 believe-and-achieve bestselling book and DVD, was directly inspired by a 1910 book only an American could have written: *The Science of Getting Rich* by Wallace D. Wattles.

As the century progressed, scholars and historians of emotion would notice that in America, virtually all sentiments except cheerfulness started to get a bad rap. Christina Kotchemidova breaks it down like this:

> Romantic love became a subject of ridicule with the liberalization of the body and the sexualization of desire. Anger came to be seen as "aggressiveness," which civilization had made inadmissible. Fear was found to be traumatizing and was minimized in the school exam system. Grief was tuned down with the rise of social care and the hospitalization of death. Mother love was said to produce "Mama's boys" and to incapacitate children. Jealousy became a sign of weakness and with the rise of indi-

vidual freedom, was socially sanctioned as a form of "possessiveness," and so forth . . . The American etiquette obliged everyone to be nice and "niceness" excluded strong emotionality. Emotional restraint was advocated across the board amounting to what Peter Stearns has called "American cool."

Joy was practically the only discrete emotion that remained positive.

But we didn't want to be *too* joyful. We were still good Puritans. The goal was not to get swept up in happiness but to exude good cheer, to be pleasant, and to smile. *Always smile.*

Don't have a college education? If you're cheerful enough, you might not need one. The sunshine spirit of the ideal Victorian wife soon found its way into the workplace. To beat the competition, salesmen had to learn to be pleasant. "Smile school" was introduced on American railroads in the 1930s. Dale Carnegie's 1936 classic, *How to Win Friends and Influence People*, taught that smiles and kindness were the best tools in both business and social life. Over the years, the book sold more than fifteen million copies.

The radio dramas in the 1940s brought with them a uniquely American invention: the laugh track. Amusement was important and, apparently, we had to be instructed when and where to express it. The laugh track would be an integral part of American television in the 1950s. In his article "A Short History of the Laugh Track," Ben Glenn II waxes nostalgic: "Over the years, having watched rerun after rerun, we all have come to know and love those nameless laughers whose voices we recognize, and who can always be counted on to assure our amusement." The funny thing is that in the drama of television, no other emotion seems to need to be assured. There are no cry tracks.

In the early 1950s, the Christian minister Norman Vincent

Peale penned a little book called *The Power of Positive Thinking*. Americans ate it up. It stayed on the *New York Times* bestseller list for more than three and a half years, sold some twenty million copies, and was ultimately translated into dozens of languages. Peale encouraged us all to make it "a habit to be happy." He advocated repeated self-hypnosis—or affirmation—as the key to harnessing divine power. No more negative thinking for you. Easier said than done, perhaps, but the good minister made it sound simple. He cofounded *Guideposts*, a monthly magazine full of inspirational stories. More than half a century later, it's one of the largest paid-circulation magazines in the country. "Empty pockets never held anyone back," Peale insisted. "Only empty heads and empty hearts can do that."

A survey of 1950s women's magazines reminds us that women were expected to be the cheeriest of the cheerful. Betty Friedan chronicled the media image of that happy smiling housewife in *The Feminine Mystique*. The message from the media was simple: no matter what's going on in your life or in the world, the answer is always *cheer up*.

And then there is that most American of icons, the yellow smiley face. The year was 1963, and State Mutual Life Assurance in Worcester, Massachusetts, had a little problem. A company merger had hurt employee morale. So managers came up with an idea—they'd start a "friendship campaign" and encourage workers to smile more. They hired the graphic designer Harvey Ball and paid him forty-five dollars to design a logo. He drew a simple smile with two eyes and made the background a cheery sunshine yellow. Ball might have become a rich man if he'd thought to trademark his work. In 1970, the brothers Murray and Bernard Spain added the phrase "Have a happy day," copyrighted the words and image, and made millions selling buttons, cards, key chains, and cookie jars emblazoned with the smiley face.

In her study of airline culture first published in the early 1980s, Arlie Russell Hochschild describes the "relax and smile training" that had become a part of the professional education. Delta Airlines trained flight attendants to cheer up one another as well as the passengers. Like the old Victorian marriage guides, training manuals encouraged flight attendants to cultivate a smile that shone "from the inside out." According to Johni Smith, the author of *How to Be a Flight Stewardess or Steward*, "The best part of a flight attendant's job is sharing her enthusiasm with new-found friends."

Today, a quick keyword search for "cheerful" on any number of Internet job sites turns up hundreds of positions—from line cook to dental assistant to bank teller to school portrait photographer. A smile gets the job done.

The International Student Federation at Saint Louis University actually cautions foreign students about American friendliness in a cultural primer, saying, "If an American seems friendly it does not necessarily mean that she/he has developed a friendship with you." It's sort of heartbreaking to imagine the kinds of misunderstandings that inspired the warning. The pamphlet goes on: "As is probably true in your culture, friendships are developed over a period of time. Although Americans may refer to classmates as friends, often they are acquaintances rather than true friends."

So what's the harm in a little cheerful friendliness, even if we don't really mean it? Hochschild wonders about the false self we create when we turn happiness on and off like a light, when we use emotion as a commodity in the workplace. As women, we were taught to use our emotions at home, too, as a service to our families. We were taught that a cheerful, nurturing mother-wife would make our loved ones feel safe. True happiness and love were preferable, of course, but we were trained to set the emotional mood even if that meant ignoring our genuine feelings.

But here's the trouble: the manufacture of happiness actually leads to emotional burnout. There's an ironic correlation between forced cheerfulness and depression. And when cheerfulness is considered the rule, even ordinary sadness or frustration—feelings that would be considered normal in many other cultures and at many other times in history—can easily be interpreted as illness.

Delta Airlines, which institutionalized positive emotional management in the 1970s, now spends nine million dollars a year paying for antidepressants for its employees and their dependents.

Hochschild writes, "When the product—the thing to be engineered, mass-produced, and subjected to speed-up and slow-down—is a smile, a mood, a feeling, or a relationship, it comes to belong to the organization and less to the self. And so in the country that most publicly celebrates the individual, more people privately wonder, without tracing the question to its deepest social root: What do I really feel?"

In his short story "Love Is a Thing on Sale for More Money Than There Exists," the New York writer Tao Lin imagines a scenario not too far from plausible: "The president brought out graphs on TV, pointed at them. He reminded the people that he was not an evil man, that he, of course, come on now—he just wanted everyone to be happy! In bed, he contemplated the abolition of both anger and unhappiness, the outlawing of them. Could he do that? Did he have the resources? Why hadn't he thought of this before?"

As Americans, we've been taught that it is our right—in fact our duty—to pursue happiness. Our attainment of happiness has been used to measure our success and personal worth. As women, we've been conditioned to see it as our job to set the emotional tone in our families, our relationships, our workplaces, and our sporting arenas. We've been told by a thousand doctors, psychologists, advertisers, and career coaches what we should do if we want to be happy. Failing that, we've learned how to *look* happy.

THE SECOND QUESTION
What could make you happier?

✸

In *Stumbling on Happiness*, the Harvard psychologist Daniel Gilbert argues that even though we humans are the only species that thinks about the future, we're lousy at predicting how we'll feel when we get there. We all want to be happy, but we look for happiness in all the wrong places. Still, I suspect we're usually better than the "experts" at knowing what we need. Before I turned to the positive psychologists, I asked women themselves: What could make you happier?

I have a lot of survival anxiety, so when I have some money, I feel better. I think if I had enough money and some medical insurance, I could be happy.

More money.

Professional stability.

Following through on all the projects I start.

More time to make art.

More hours in the day.

More time to myself.

Moving back to the city.

Moving to Vermont and having a farm.

Time to exercise.

A good night's sleep.

Maybe just a little nap.

Being twenty pounds lighter.

To stop thinking I need to lose weight.

More sex.

This is going to sound very antifeminist and kind of clingy, but I often wish I had a real partner—someone who supported what I do as an artist and as an activist but also had their own interests that dovetail or complement my own work without competing with it. In my ideal partnership, we could work on our separate projects in the same space without feeling uncomfortable, stifled, or ignored.

Love.

Children.

Grandchildren.

I would be happier if I thought my children were happier.

A little less time in airports and more time at home.

If I could lose this sense of pending doom.

I think spirituality is the key.

More dancing.

Less stress.

Isn't that THE question?

I am happy! That's like asking a rich person how they could be richer.

prescriptions for contentment

✺

*Just as I am turning thirty-five, I find myself having some trouble
with happiness. I feel overwhelmed with life, exhausted. I love my
work, my family—in some ways I'm the happiest I've ever been. But
in other ways I feel stuck, like life is passing me by and I am not getting done the things I should get done. Is this depression or just part
of the natural ebb and flow?*

—FROM SONJA'S JOURNAL

In late summer, my daughter packs up sixty-five pairs of shoes
and a few other essential possessions and heads south for her first
year of college. At age seventeen, she's never been away from
home for more than a few weeks. The city where she'll set up
house is smog-covered Los Angeles—vast and alienating. The
school she has chosen provides neither dorms nor communal
dining and is well-known for its tough first-year curriculum. In
the early weeks, I watch the morning weather reports that
promise only sunshine for Los Angeles, but every night my
daughter cries on the phone.

A month into the school year, she's still homesick, over-
whelmed with work, and starting to fall behind. "I thought I
would feel grown-up when I moved to L.A.," she whispers. "But
I just feel little all the time."

"Why don't you go talk to your adviser at school," I suggest. "That's what she's there for."

My daughter hesitates. She doesn't have time, she says. She doesn't think it will do any good, she says. But she finally agrees to make the appointment.

"The adviser was nice enough," my daughter tells me later, "but what do you think she suggested?"

Perhaps you can guess.

Did the adviser . . .

(*a*) reach out in empathy and acknowledge that it must be difficult to leave home, adjust to life in the second-largest city in America, and get swallowed in more schoolwork than a girl ever knew existed?

(*b*) point my daughter to existing academic resources on campus, like school tutoring?

(*c*) refer her to a counselor to talk about all these things? Or did she . . .

(*d*) refer her to a counselor "to see if you need to be on anti-depressant medication"?

Yep. That adviser, who wasn't a doctor and who'd met my daughter all of once, suggested that the answer to being over-whelmed by a major life transition was to take a mood-altering drug.

What's up with the baby boomers and their drugs?

"Maybe you're clinically depressed," I conceded on the phone that afternoon. "Or maybe you're seventeen and you just moved to L.A."

The counselor, to his credit, offered my daughter a jour-nal rather than a bottle of pills, and the adviser eventually became an ally, but that adviser's initial reaction to a young woman's anxiety and sadness says a lot about where we're at as a culture. Medicate first, ask questions later.

As a new college student, my daughter wasn't alone. According to the American College Health Association, the percentage of college students diagnosed with depression has increased 56 percent since 2001. And even back in 2001, *USA Today* was reporting that "mental illness is absolutely going off the charts on college campuses."

Modern psychopharmacology has allowed millions of people with serious mental illnesses to lead normal lives, but psychology has become a science steeped in illness ideology, and as a result we've become wildly overmedicated.

"The stringencies of managed care," Martin Seligman writes in his afterword to *A Life Worth Living*, edited by Mihaly Csikszentmihalyi and Isabella Selega Csikszentmihalyi, have "seduced clinical psychology and psychiatry into working only on symptom relief and not on cures, creating a profession of firefighters."

The result: about half of all Americans are taking at least one prescription drug—making us the most medicated country on earth. Each year, over 200 million antidepressant prescriptions are dispensed in the United States. In 2004 alone, some 1.6 million children and teenagers—280,000 of them under age ten—were given two or more psychiatric drugs in combination.

So much for "Just Say No."

According to the World Health Organization, just being female is a significant predictor for being prescribed a mood-altering psychotropic drug. The most common of those drugs is, of course, the antidepressant. But what is this illness we're treating with all these drugs? What most of us know about depression boils down to conventional wisdom and personal experience. Here's what I thought I knew about it:

- Depression is a complex illness with psychological and biological causes.
- The rate of depression is twice as high among women as it is among men.
- I had twice been diagnosed with it. The first time I had no insurance and no cash on hand, so I was sent on my unmerry way with my diagnosis and a referral to a low-income clinic that no longer existed. The second time I was prescribed an antidepressant. When I had a severe allergic reaction, I quit taking the drug and refused to try another. I discovered in those gasping allergic moments, as my heart rate stampeded ahead of my thoughts, that I valued my ability to breathe. The realization that I'd rather be depressed than dead came as a welcome surprise. I secretly wondered if that wasn't the magic of the pill—to show me how bad I could really feel so I might come to appreciate my relatively ordinary despair.

As for *why* depression affected more women than men, I'd read a hundred different theories. The most popular explanations pointed to hormones, societal inequalities, and a feminine tendency to silence ourselves in relationships. All plausible enough, but the hormonal theory sounded an awful lot like that wandering uterus all over again. If the problem was social inequities, the obvious solution would be societal change. If our trouble was rooted in the way we've been conditioned to surrender our will in relationships, the answer might lie in personal empowerment. But, alas, the primary treatments for depression are not herbs known to promote hormonal balance, social change, or even talk therapy, but drugs designed to "normalize" our brain chemistries.

All this I knew as I set out to discover how we got here, with the hope of illuminating the great *why* of depression's gender gap. All this I knew, but it's a good thing I was prepared to find myself a fool. Everything I knew wasn't wrong, exactly, but I might have been wise to consider the source of all my knowledge.

Depression is real. It has existed since humans developed language to complain about it. We can find descriptions of "melancholia" in Greek medical texts, in the Bible, and in Chinese mythology. But depression as we now know it—the illness considered by many to be the common cold of psychology—was born just a few generations ago.

The year was 1952. *I Love Lucy* was the number-one show on television. Senator Joe McCarthy was busy running around the country making speeches about the evils of communism. The first edition of the American Psychiatric Association's *Diagnostic and Statistical Manual* (*DSM-I*) was published—but it didn't mention depression as a specific disease. As healthy Americans laughed at Lucy and Ethel's antics, something historic was taking place in Staten Island, New York. At Sea View Hospital, with its beautiful terra-cotta murals depicting "mankind's joys and sorrows," nearly a hundred tuberculosis patients received an experimental drug treatment called Marsilid. The new medication was a derivative of hydrazine, a chemical the Germans had used at the end of World War II to power their V-2 rockets.

Boom!

The experiment was a smashing success. The drug not only cleared up the TB patients' lung problems, but it had the amazing and unexpected side effect of inducing euphoria. Rumor had it those patients were dancing in the wards.

Marsilid might have made the perfect street drug—pushers could have promised instant ecstasy—but the researchers who discovered this upper had a better idea. *What if there was an actual illness we could treat with this rocket fuel?*

What if?

A 1957 ad for Marsilid would promise near-universal success rates in treating schizophrenia, personality disorders, and manic depression, but these major psychiatric illnesses were rare in the general population. What scientists and drugmakers needed was something commonplace, something they could really market to the masses as the next big thing . . .

Something *epidemic.*

When they found that Marsilid prevented the brain from breaking down serotonin, an interesting little neurotransmitter that had recently been discovered, they had it. Depression wasn't some psychological or existential mood, they decided, it was a bona fide brain disease caused by "serotonin deficiency."

Most diseases are observed and defined *before* doctors start looking for a cure. Not so with "serotonin deficiency." The introduction of Marsilid and other medications that would come to be known as "antidepressants" actually *resulted* in the concept of depression as a specific disease. Pharmaceutical companies designed their own studies and analyzed their own findings. With each new insight, they expanded or altered their definition of depression to include the symptoms the drugs seemed to treat and exclude the symptoms they didn't.

If you were a doctor in the late 1950s or early 1960s and you hadn't heard of "serotonin deficiency," you soon would. Drug companies spread the word like gospel. The pharmaceutical company Merck went so far as to buy fifty thousand copies of the otherwise-obscure book *Recognizing the Depressed Patient* by Frank Ayd, one of the doctors who'd pioneered the serotonin theory. According to Ayd, who wrote in layman's terms for the nonpsychiatrist, depression wasn't just a disease for the asylums—it was something that could be diagnosed on general medical wards and in primary care offices. Merck distributed the book to doctors who might not have heard the news: depression was the disease for which these fine new drugs were the cure.

In stark contrast to most clinical trials that tested drugs on only male subjects, most of the subjects for studies on depression were female. The difference went unquestioned until later decades when researchers explained it away by saying that women suffered more depression than men. But back in the 1950s, patients weren't chosen for these studies based on their diagnoses—there was no real diagnosis for depression. So why were women suddenly the go-to guinea pigs?

"Researchers studied hospitalized depressed women, counted their symptoms, and then used them to define a category of depression. The question of whether women were depressed more than men was never raised," writes Laura D. Hirshbein, a professor of psychiatry at the University of Michigan. "Thus the connection between women and depression has been a closed circle: researchers have assumed that women are depressed more than men, which means that women have been preferentially diagnosed, treated, and theorized about, leading to further conclusions that women are depressed more than men."

Women may have been chosen for the studies because psychiatric wards housed more women than men at the time, or because researchers didn't want to try their drugs on self-proclaimed alcoholics (which would have excluded more men than women), or perhaps it had more to do with drug companies' bottom line. A woman's role as the cheerful "sunshine of the circle around her" had by now become deeply rooted in American culture. Any failure to emanate that sunshine had come to be seen as abnormal—even disturbed. Consciously or unconsciously, researchers may have been more likely to see a woman's melancholy as cause for concern. Maybe it was clear that women would be more likely to seek psychiatric treatment not only for immobilizing depression but also for ordinary lack of cheerfulness. Maybe women were, from the get-go, the drug-makers' target market.

Most physical and mental illnesses are defined by their observable symptoms, but modern depression has been described and defined based on the patients' own reporting of how they feel. Since more women were studied, their descriptions became the definition of the disease. So even women's unique emotional language has played a part in reinforcing the idea that this "disease" is, basically, a chick thing.

By the 1970s, the assumption that depression was for women had become so entrenched that studies done entirely on women were reported as studies on depression itself. One by one, symptoms like irritability, hostility, and denial of illness—all more common among men—were removed from the diagnostic criteria for depression. When researchers were ready to "prove" that depression struck more women than men—that fully two-thirds of people suffering from it were female—they failed to mention that the exact same proportion of research subjects had been women.

Still, drugmakers had succeeded in finding their epidemic. By 1975, the concept of depression in both men and women had become so common that Robert Woodruff, a prominent psychiatric researcher at Washington University in St. Louis, would ask, "Is everyone depressed?"

The 1980 edition of the American Psychiatric Association's *Diagnostic and Statistical Manual* (*DSM-III*) finally listed depression as a distinct mental illness. The formal diagnostic criteria gave depression that lucrative mark of approval: the five-digit code that allows doctors to bill insurance companies for treatment. Maybe it was pure coincidence, but that same edition of the diagnostic manual was the first to exclude "hysteria."

The current *Diagnostic and Statistical Manual (DSM-IV)* lists nine symptoms of depression: sadness, diminished pleasure, weight gain or loss, insomnia or excessive sleeping, behavior that's either agitated or slowed down, fatigue, guilt, trouble concentrating, and recurrent thoughts of death. For a diagnosis of major depression, a patient needs five of the nine symptoms, but there's a sneaky little "provisional diagnosis" listed in the back of the book, where it awaits further study. It's called "minor depression," and it requires only two of the listed symptoms. If everyone wasn't depressed in 1975, we sure will be if "minor depression" ever gains full disease status. Ever put on ten pounds and felt guilty? *We have a diagnosis for that.*

I recently heard Charles Barber, the author of *Comfortably Numb: How Psychiatry Is Medicating a Nation*, on NPR. He described a debilitating obsessive-compulsive disorder that kept him up nights his first year of college repeating words for hours. Few of us would argue that his level of fear was of medical concern. But what of common sadness? None of the women on my council of experts appeared to be suffering from "major depression," but all reported down days. "I don't feel unhappy," Roslyn wrote. "I just have this low-lying level of sadness and some loneliness."

"Just happy that this day is over," Jennifer noted. "Too much. Too long. Head full. Need to sleep. Happy that I didn't break down."

"I feel sad sometimes," Sonja wrote. "A lot of anger is bubbling up. I'm not getting the love I want, broke, no alone time."

Should we consider these sentiments disease?

Here we are, living in a culture that has deemed virtually

every emotion except joy to be negative, and we're on the verge of defining virtually any sign of being in a funk as mental illness.

The evidence for the serotonin theory was circumstantial to begin with, and more than fifty years later it remains pretty sketchy. Despite decades of research designed by the drug companies themselves, the treatments for depression barely meet American medical standards. Far from the hoped-for universal success, in more than half of the clinical trials used to approve the current leading antidepressants, the drugs have failed to outperform placebos. And, as it turns out, for up to 50 percent of patients, antidepressants don't work at all.

Even for those of us who are helped by antidepressants, the results are admittedly cosmetic; the drugs treat the symptoms without curing the disease. If they provide us the energy to make necessary life changes or to get us through particularly dangerous passages, or if they help us to reduce our fear to a manageable level, they have served us, but if we're chronically depressed and can only look forward to a lifetime of prescriptions, we have to wonder.

To say that something is an invention isn't to say that it's a myth. Depression is real. Modern depression is more real for women than it is for men precisely because it's one of the few conditions that has been defined by women's experience of it. Depression is worth our healing attention. But considering the history of depression as we know it, the mind does wander. What if medical researchers had stumbled on a drug that caused people to become pacifists instead of can-do optimists? Might they have been able to market nonviolence with the same zeal with which they've marketed good cheer? What if drug companies had foreseen huge profits in the possibility of ending violence and war? What if the emotional culture and market economy had demanded "peace pills" for men instead of "happy pills" for women? The "common cold" of psychology might easily have become dominance and aggression rather than depression.

I'm just saying.

When we throw around concepts like "Women are twice as likely as men to be depressed," we should remember that depression isn't some God-sent illness—and it isn't the opposite of happiness. Depression is a summary of the way women have described feeling when we hit a particularly dark and immobilizing emotional knot.

When my daughter went off to college, she experienced that knot away from her family and community of friends. She sought support and found, instead, advice that combined the traditional American "Chin up!" attitude with the new American penchant for mood-altering medication.

Four months into the school year, my daughter came home for a visit, feeling better. I made jalapeño mac 'n' cheese, and we sat on our big red couch while she told me about Los Angeles. "I could have got those antidepressants so easily," she said, "but you know, I didn't want them. I wanted to try to deal with it, right? And you know what really helped me in the end? I don't know if you're going to get it. Maybe this doesn't make sense if you don't live in L.A. But someone, I don't know who, they put these little pieces of Scotch tape up around the parking structure at school. They put these pieces of tape right at eye level on the concrete walls and in the elevator, and on those pieces of tape they just wrote, 'Everything's going to be OK.' There aren't that many of them, but whenever I was really stressed-out, whenever my teacher had just told me I'd done everything wrong or I had to go get new supplies and redo my whole design project in forty-five minutes, that's when I'd see a little piece of tape.

'Everything's going to be OK.' Just this homemade thing. One person reaching out. That never happens in L.A. And I wonder if the person who made those pieces of tape knows. Just reaching out like that. Saying, you know, someone else has felt like that. It saved my life."

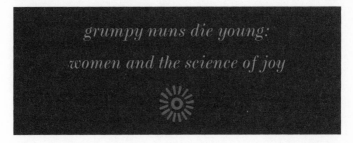

grumpy nuns die young:
women and the science of joy

If we go into a darkened room and turn on the light, it doesn't matter if the room has been dark for a day, a week, or ten thousand years—we turn on the light and it is illuminated. Once we control our capacity for love and happiness, the light has been turned on.

—SHARON SALZBERG

happiness is a potato

❂

It's a baby! I thought this pregnancy would never end, but the labor itself was quick and surreal. I remember everything hot-cold. And the lights. And now him! To touch his skin, his little nose, his little mouth. To wake to his wide eyes. He is bright like the morning.

—FROM ARIEL'S JOURNAL

The ancient Greeks attributed happiness to being favored by the gods. A spin of the universal wheel and you were dealt your disposition. Their fatalism is captured in our language: the English words for happiness, happenstance, haphazard, and hapless all derive from the same root—the Old Norse *happ*, meaning "luck" or "chance."

"No mockery in this world ever sounds to me so hollow as that of being told to *cultivate* happiness," Charlotte Brontë wrote. "What does such advice mean? Happiness is not a potato, to be planted in mould, and tilled with manure."

Happiness, our cultural and linguistic traditions tell us, just *happens*. But much of what we do in life, our motivation stripped down to its essence, is with the hope of cultivating happiness. So which is it? Chance—ephemeral and improbable—or something we can intentionally plant and till?

I remember a rainy morning years ago. I drove across the San Francisco Bay Bridge in my beat-up Dodge Colt. That old car rode like a dirt bike and sounded like a leaf blower. Through the pebble-cracked windshield, I checked out the cars around me. They were new. They were luxurious and comfortable—I could just tell. They purred along, arrogant as cats. I imagined all those cars had heaters and plush interiors. I imagined they had stereos on which both the tuner and the volume worked. I thought the drivers of those cars looked entitled and blasé as they passed me by. They didn't know how lucky they were. If I were ever blessed with a shiny car, I thought, I would know just how lucky I was. I would appreciate what I had. I don't ask for much, I thought, just a nice, warm, reliable car. That would make me happy.

A few years later, I got just what I'd dreamed of. Shiny and red. I was ecstatic. My mother told me that I was the first woman in our family ever to buy her own car. *The first!* It wasn't a brand-new car, but it had fewer than 100,000 miles on it, and it was new to me. I drove that thing around like I owned the free-ways. I turned up the stereo. I blasted the heater. I didn't worry about roadside breakdowns or getting pulled over for missing lights or missing registration stickers. I appreciated what I had.

And then . . .

After about two weeks . . .

I got used to it.

I wouldn't have traded the new Honda for the old Dodge, but the magic had worn off. I accelerated past the beaters, oblivious to my privilege. That shiny red car, in all its reliable glory, ceased to have any impact on my day-to-day emotional life. Folks who study this kind of thing call it "hedonic adaptation."

My own personal happiness thermostat regulated my good cheer back to blasé entitlement. My thermostat's set range: fair to middling.

We all fantasize that some life change will cheer us up—permanently. We'll get rich, get skinny, get some new and improved gadget in the office, or we'll get swept off our glass-slippered feet and get married. We'll then live as the fairy tale promises, happily ever after. But hedonic adaptation theory—or the "hedonic treadmill"—reminds us that we respond not so much to permanent conditions as to change. Most people have a "set point" or "set range" for happiness, the theory says, and that range is set not by the circumstances of our lives—not by shiny red cars or noisy clunkers—but by our natural genetic disposition. Some people will never be particularly happy. Each of us has a set point—contented or grumpy. When something amazing happens to us, we don't cheer up for good. Instead, we cheer up, get used to it, and then return to our previous set level of happiness. It's the change up that thrills us, not our new status. If something life shattering happens, on the other hand, we get bummed out—but eventually we accept our new lot in life and start thinking *The Daily Show* is pretty funny again.

On the first springtime sunny day in the gray city where I live, everyone you meet smiles so friendly you'd think you were living in Mr. Rogers's neighborhood. Not so in Los Angeles, where another cloudless seventy-five-degree day is, well, just another cloudless seventy-five-degree day. And everyone's still stuck in traffic.

The proof for the theory of hedonic adaptation lies in a widely cited 1978 study of lottery winners and paraplegics that found that both tended to revert to their previous level of good cheer or grumpiness within a year following the event that changed their lives. A team of psychologists at Northwestern University interviewed twenty-two Illinois State Lottery winners and compared them with twenty-two people selected randomly from the phone book. The average windfall was about a half-million dollars—seven had won a million dollars each. After their initial happy surprise, the winners were no happier than the random sample of their fellow citizens. In fact, the lottery winners' pleasure in everyday activities like talking to friends, eating breakfast, or reading a magazine actually dropped. The same psychologists studied twenty-nine accident victims who had lost the use of their arms or legs. The findings were symmetrical to the findings in the lottery winner study. The accident victims rated their happiness a bit lower than those selected from the phone book—still quite positively on the happiness scale— but they expected to be just as happy in the not-distant future.

What does all this say about those of us who actively seek happiness? And what does it say about our prospects? Are we doomed to spend our lives pining away in vain after the love we hear about in pop songs, the wealth of bronzed celebrities, or the enlightened bliss of Buddhist nuns? Would none of these things make the least bit of difference? Are we wasting our time with all this pursuit?

Positive psychologists have tried to look on the sunny side of hedonic adaptation theory. *Within* our natural set range, they've argued, we can train ourselves to be happier and more optimistic. We can build lives that support our basic contentment. But how valid is the concept of a set range, anyway? Maybe I'd been mistaken about how much I really wanted or needed a more comfortable car. Maybe it was the commute to the unpaid internship that was getting me down. Maybe I'd have been better off with a sparkly banana-seat bicycle. Positive psychology has long held that money doesn't buy happiness, so the lottery winner example might not tell us much. And while the *average* level of happiness among paraplegics may return to its starting point, a lot of folks with disabilities and major illnesses do suffer from chronic depression—alternately, some 30 to 40 percent actually report a *higher* quality of life than the general population, finding new meaning in life through the shock and daily challenge of adversity.

The theory of hedonic adaptation was recently challenged when Richard E. Lucas, a professor of psychology at Michigan State University, decided to do a study of his own. Lucas had gotten to thinking: those famous lottery winner and spinal cord injury studies relied on subjects who were chosen *after* their windfall or accident—so they were being asked to recall how happy they'd been before. This time, Lucas and his colleagues used data from Germany and Great Britain that captured levels of life satisfaction both prior to and after major life events. They discovered that we can get used to some things better than others. Most of us adapt pretty quickly to marriage, for example. We're super-excited when we first get hitched, but after a few fights over the recycling and a few disappointing Christmas presents we're back to our previous levels of happiness or misery. We can mostly adapt if our spouse drops dead, too, but this takes longer—about seven years on average (perhaps depending on how bad those Christmas presents were). But divorce is another story. Divorce can seriously mess with our heads. Many of us never get back to our previous level of happiness, even if we remarry. The same is true for unemployment. Even after we find a new job, we don't bounce back. There has been some fundamental blow to our self-esteem, and that takes a toll.

"Happiness levels do change, adaptation is not inevitable, and life events do matter," Lucas concluded.

Not surprisingly, there's a gender difference when it comes to our reactions to divorce and unemployment. Love and bread-winning are gendered narratives. As women, we were taught to find our self-worth in love relationships. Twentieth-century men were conditioned to believe that if they couldn't support a wife and children, they were losers. So it is that women have a harder time adapting to the end of a marriage, and men take it harder when they find themselves out of work. It's not the relationship or the job itself so much as the loss of something we've invested our egos in. Proponents of the set-point theory of happiness argue that these events have somehow served to *reset* our happiness thermostats. But if our thermostats can be reset, wouldn't it be just as easy to argue that there was no set point to begin with? No natural genetic disposition?

A few years after I got my shiny red car, I found myself depressed again—and with every righteous reason in the world to be so. I was a single mom earning money for the first time in my life and spending almost all of it defending myself in an ugly child custody battle. I was a traveler forbidden by the court to leave the county I lived in because even though I'd never defied a judge's order, the family court mediator tagged me as a "flight risk." The nightly news recounted tragedy after human tragedy, and I just couldn't seem to quit smoking. After my severe allergic reaction to the antidepressant Wellbutrin, I complained to an acquaintance—a well-known musician and mom who suffered from bipolar disorder—that I felt doomed to my misery. Surely she would understand my sense of helplessness in the face of an endless bad day. But she shook her head and told me something that would set my mind in motion: "Happiness is hard work."

Work?

I'd never thought of it that way.

I heard her words echoed a few years later when happenstance found me sitting in a bleacher in Kansas City listening to the medical clown and social activist Patch Adams introduce a documentary about a group of clowns who visited Afghanistan after the U.S. invasion. Robin Williams's movie portrayal of the good doctor hadn't prepared me for the effervescent wild man I'd spotted leaping across a sunny college campus earlier that afternoon. Mesmerized by the odd grace of his stride, I'd followed him to this gymnasium lecture venue. He'd been hospitalized for depression three times before he turned eighteen, he told the audience. He'd been suicidal because he didn't want to live in a world of violence and injustice. But on his last visit to the psych ward, he made a decision: he would never have another bad day. "I decided to love life," he said.

Decided?

Happiness, Patch Adams and my musician acquaintance seemed to be saying, could be an act of will, a discipline. Even if our natural dispositions weren't easily joyful, we didn't have to settle for some fated spin of the wheel. We could choose happiness—and we could get to work on its cultivation. Their assertion harked back to the New Agers of my childhood who told me I created my own reality, but these two seemed to speak with a more soulful authority—and without the victim-blaming undertone. My bipolar musician friend was well acquainted with the dark night of the human psyche. Patch Adams had seen the landscapes of war. In the midst of suffering, these two were making a conscious effort to rejoice.

Set-point theories, then, need to be interpreted not as the limit of our potential but as a starting place. We're each born with different temperaments, different personalities. The idea that kids are "blank slates" waiting to be written upon by parents and teachers is wacky—largely the work of the seventeenth-century British philosopher John Locke, a fellow who obviously didn't spend much time caring for infants.

From their first waking moments in this world I could see that my son, Maximilian, and my daughter, Maia, were very different kids. They started out different and they will remain different, but they're not *totally* at the mercy of their genetic destinies. They're maybe *50 percent* at the mercy of their genetic destinies.

Indeed, studies of twins and adoptees show us that about 50 percent of a person's sense of well-being is determined from birth—by our nature.

The experimental psychologist Sonja Lyubomirsky claims that another 10 percent of our happiness can be attributed to life circumstances—and she was probably pretty happy when she got a million-dollar grant from the National Institute of Mental Health to study it all. But what about the remaining 40 percent? Lyubomirsky and other scientists now believe that fully 40 percent of our happiness is under our control and depends on "intentional activities"—mental and behavioral strategies we can use to counteract adaptation's downward pull. Even if our glasses are more than half-empty, 40 percent happiness isn't nothing. Forty percent happiness is something we can work with. Forty percent happiness might even be enough to ensure that we never have another bad day.

If happiness is hard work, I decide, I've got plenty of it in front of me—but my goal is clear and my heart is pure. If my set range for happiness is fair to middling, I hereby reject my set range. Happiness is a potato, I prefer to think, and I've cultivated a potato or two in my day.

THE THIRD QUESTION
What is your fondest memory?

✺

When I asked a hundred women to share their fondest memories, they thought of sweet accomplishments, rites of passage, simple moments in time—an instant or an afternoon when they were neither hungry nor afraid and they were able to connect with another person or with nature.

Walking in the Colorado mountains with a babysitter when I was four years old. I remember the vanilla smell of ponderosa pines, clear little streams to wade in, catching grasshoppers, and big crazy fields of mountain wildflowers.

Sitting in the car with my godmother eating Svenhard's pastries with lunch meat on them before I went to the babysitter after kindergarten.

When my mother spoon-fed me a soft boiled egg at barely nine years old when I was about to depart alone on an international trip and was too nervous to actually eat the egg myself. My mother was always a very loving person, but this moment is etched in my heart.

Going ice-skating with my father on a Sunday afternoon when I was ten, then out to dinner with both my parents to their favorite restaurant, Ruby Foo's.

Walking home from a drugstore Christmas-shopping trip with my mother and three sisters in the falling snow about thirty years ago.

Running away from home when I was seventeen and late at night under the stars realizing I was a whole and independent person and the world would take care of me and my parents' world was small and lonely and it didn't have to be my own.

It used to be like Saturday Night Fever *out on the dance floor for me. On my twenty-first birthday, with all my friends around, the spotlight was on me for "Dancing Queen" and I didn't care what anybody thought.*

That giddy time right after I met and hooked up with someone new— laughing at a lot of the same silly things and sharing stories about our lives.

Throwing bales of hay off the back of a four-wheeler to the rescued animals at a farm sanctuary.

Getting the notice that I won the New York Foundation for the Arts Award.

Riding the waves in Puerto Escondido.

Being pregnant with my daughter and just hiking all day and picking berries.

Labor ending, and my daughter being placed on my belly.

When my son was little and still a bit pudgy and sweaty and clingy.

An uncrowded day on the beach with my five-year-old daughter last summer. We happily wallowed in the day from late morning to sunset. Breezy and just warm enough. I'd remembered to bring everything we needed—food, drinks, toys, books, sunscreen, change of clothes, towels, a tent for shade and napping. We just played. I suddenly wished that I'd brought a kite, and then a SpongeBob SquarePants kite washed up on the beach—still connected to its string and handle. We call it "The Miracle of the Kite."

Walking my son to school and looking up at the sky and thinking, "This is what I've always wanted."

Meeting the son I gave up for adoption for the first (second) time.

Drinking by the river with a friend on a sunny day.

Having sushi with my boyfriend and listening to Tom Waits.

Being in Santa Fe with three girlfriends at a Japanese-style spa high in the mountains. We all had massages, then sat in the hot tub and watched the full lunar eclipse.

toward a general theory of positive emotions

✲

I'm alive. I feel like crying and it's okay. Rawness is to be expected. My teacher stares at me pointedly. I'm an ideal student: authentic, receptive, and open, and she's affecting me. My soul needs the replenishment of this class. I seriously couldn't have a better school experience.

—FROM LINDA'S JOURNAL

Let's forget about "American cool" for a little while—that notion that emotional restraint is part of who we are.

For the sake of argument, let's reject the notion that our emotions need to be dulled.

Let's dismiss the concept that feelings are irrational—a chick thing. *She's so emotional*, we say, meaning that she shouldn't be taken seriously and, by extension, that we shouldn't take our own emotions seriously.

Let's entertain the possibility that emotions are basically good. Let's imagine that they serve a purpose. Let's consider that emotions are our body and our mind and our psychology telling us what's going on and preparing us for what to do next.

Traditional theories of emotion have focused on the constrictive feelings we consider negative—like anger, disgust, and fear. And why wouldn't they focus on those? Not only can negative emotions lead to serious trouble when they get out of hand, but their *helpful* role in our lives is also pretty easy to understand. Our survival as a species has depended on our quick ability to get ourselves out of life-or-death situations. Anger prepares us to attack. Disgust prompts us to spit out what's not good for us. Fear prepares us to escape—our bodies react by redirecting blood to large muscle groups so we can run. Even anxiety has its utility, helping us to imagine every worst-case scenario and avoid disaster. Some of the positive emotions make simple sense, too. Pleasure is useful insofar as we've evolved to enjoy the things we need—like food and sex. But what about joy beyond physical satisfaction? The role of positive emotions has been harder for evolutionary psychologists to grasp. Optimism and contentment don't do us much good when a mountain lion has us by the throat. Aristotle figured that happiness was an end state, the goal of goals and our reward for living a virtuous life, but the University of North Carolina psychology professor Barbara Fredrickson thinks it's a bit more complicated than that. First of all, positive emotions *do* inspire necessary action. Joy sparks our urge to play, interest and curiosity lead us to explore, contentment relaxes us enough to savor and integrate our experiences, love inspires us to nurture and protect each other. We invent, construct, cozy up, and survive.

Positive emotions signal optimal functioning, Fredrickson says, but they also *produce* optimal functioning—and not just in the present pleasant moment but also over the long term. Negative emotions help us narrow our attention. Our pupils constrict. If we're pissed off, we can focus on the object of our anger and target our attack with the precision we need to prevail. But that tight focus only serves us up to a point. Fredrickson's broaden-and-build theory says that positive emotions do just the opposite, and they lead us to expressive and exploratory behavior that's equally important. Happiness isn't just a pleasant state of being, then; it's a dynamic force that propels us into and through our lives, compelling us to pursue knowledge, to build strong social relationships, and to create works of art and ingenuity.

In Fredrickson's lab, study participants were assigned to watch films that induced positive emotions like amusement and contentment, negative emotions like fear and sadness, or no emotions at all. Subjects were then shown drawings and asked which of two other drawings the first one most resembled. The drawings were designed so that people would give one answer if they focused on the details and another if they looked at the big picture. The results proved that positive and negative emotions do affect our perceptions. In a variation on the same experiment, students were shown the film clips and then asked to make a list of things they'd like to do. Subjects who experienced positive emotions came up with more activities and showed heightened levels of creativity. In longer-term studies, Fredrickson found that positive emotions help us build psychological resources like resilience. When we're happy, we flourish. Some creative thinkers have been famously depressed, but Fredrickson's research suggests that joy, rather than anxiety, misery, or even necessity, can be the mother of invention.

As Britt said when we met as the council of experts, "It makes me get excited about my future when I write about happiness. I feel like, Wow, this is an attainable thing. I've already come this far. I feel proud of myself. I'm smart enough to know what makes me happy, and I *almost* know what it takes to get there."

So negative emotions are important for surviving life-and-death situations, and pessimism can help us envision and avoid crummy outcomes even when the stakes aren't so high, but happiness and joy aren't just shallow or self-indulgent vacations on the beach. Positive emotions—and the focus on positive emotions—teach us to thrive.

Now, let's get back to those grumpy nuns.

In the 1930s, 180 young women wrote brief essays explaining why they wanted to become sisters. They knew their writing would be read by the mother superior, so few were overtly negative, but "you could get a feel for the person," said Deborah Danner, the psychologist who spearheaded the study three generations later. She and other researchers had come across the essays in convent archives when they were looking for material that might confirm earlier findings that linked a good vocabulary in youth to a low risk of Alzheimer's in old age. Instead, they discovered that upbeat nuns lived a full decade longer than the nuns whose language was more neutral. That's an even bigger life-expectancy difference than you'll find between smokers and nonsmokers.

So puff away—just make sure you've got a smile on your face.

Looking at the famous study, Barbara Fredrickson asked *why* the happy nuns lived longer, tinkered away in her lab for a while, and came up with something called the "undo effect." The reason positive emotions help us live longer, according to her theory, is that they curtail the health-damaging side effects of negative emotions. So say you're in crisis. You're freaking out, and your heart rate goes up. All this anxiety and adrenaline might help you deal with the situation at hand, but what happens when the crisis is over? Negative emotions have lingering effects. We're jumpy and stressed-out even after the danger has passed. While I was working on this very chapter, an old friend showed up at my door, asking for shelter. She'd been out of the country, she said, and had just arrived in town on a Greyhound bus. I hadn't seen her in years, and I thought it was strange that she averted her eyes when she spoke to me, but I told myself she was probably just road-weary or embarrassed to find herself on my doorstep. I invited her in. Of course she could stay.

There was an odd skip in her step, and when I pointed her to the extra bedroom, I noticed that she didn't have any luggage.

"Where's your backpack?" I asked.

She just covered her eyes with her hair and giggled.

She slept all day, sang angry punk rock songs all night, then walked into my kitchen at noon, downed a whole bottle of red wine, and lit her spaghetti on fire.

When I told her it was time for her to leave, she put on a pair of sunglasses.

It was cold outside, and the city was giving out emergency vouchers for motel rooms. I offered her the hotline number, but she refused. She wasn't a homeless person, she said.

For three days and three nights, I didn't sleep.

My strange guest never threatened me—she often seemed like a small and confused child—but her behavior was odd and unpredictable. I felt afraid. And I had a baby in the house. Still, I'd never before been in a position to put a young woman out on the street. So I let her stall me.

On her third night in my house, the young traveler stumbled into my room, sort of lunged toward my bed, and then collapsed onto the floor. "What are you guys doing?" she chirped, and then she started to cry. It was 3:00 a.m. Enough was enough.

In the morning, I chased her out.

I dreamed of cars without brakes and the girl from the movie *Vagabond* frozen dead in a field. A week later, my shoulders were still tense. I startled easily. I kept the front door locked now, but I could feel my heart rate quicken when I heard footsteps on the porch. It's the state of hypervigilance Fredrickson warns us about. Instead of serving to protect us, feeling constantly on guard can end up giving us a coronary.

The traveler is gone now. I should relax.

This is where positive emotions might come to the rescue. According to Fredrickson's undo hypothesis, happiness works its magic by producing a quick unwinding of pent-up tension, restoring the cardiovascular system to normal. We bounce back from stress. Some people seem to be naturally good at this recovery. The rest of us, according to Fredrickson, can deliberately harness the positive and calming emotions we need.

In Fredrickson's lab, she and a coworker told a group of student volunteers that they had just a few minutes to prepare a speech that would be videotaped and critiqued by their peers. The researchers monitored the students' heart rates and blood pressure, and, predictably, the students got nervous. After a few minutes, the psych professors let the students off the hook, telling them that they wouldn't actually have to deliver the speeches. The students were later asked how they'd felt during the experiment. Those who viewed the whole thing as amusing saw their heart rates return to normal much faster than those who were pissed off about being tricked. The lingering effects of the stress were undone by good humor. Negative emotions narrow our focus—or what Fredrickson calls our "momentary thought-action repertoire"—and positive emotions broaden this same focus or repertoire. In that broadening, the positive emotions loosen the hold the negative emotions have on our mind and body by dismantling our preparation for fight, flight, or chasing a crazy old friend out into the rain. Fredrickson hasn't identified the precise mechanisms by which all this happens, but the broaden-and-build theory suggests that "broadening at the cognitive level mediates undoing at the cardiovascular level." In other words, we open our minds to steady our hearts.

The women on my council of experts who shared their journals were all able to trace different patterns from their recorded moments of happiness. "Friends inspired me," wrote Calliope, a community health nurse in her early thirties. "Almost all my moments were in conjunction with other people." Margaret, a writer in her early forties, noted that "writing and creative work made me happy." Sonja noticed that she most often sought solace in nature and relationships. "The sun made me happy yesterday," she wrote. "The beautiful ocean at Hug Point Beach. The dogs running around. The little waterfall. My baby looking at me and smiling—so full of love. This morning it made me feel good to go swimming in the cold ocean. It made me happy to decide on a whim to stay at the beach for a second night." Jennifer, an artist, said, "My happiness usually comes from visual finds. Just today I found this smashed tulip. Many days that's what I wrote, 'I found this cool thing in the gutter.'" According to Fredrickson's theories, whatever those things are that bring us even small joy serve to heal us.

But how can we put the undo effect to use? Real life is more complicated than a psychology lab. In the case of the traveler, it's not as if I'd been punked. Barbara Fredrickson isn't going to emerge from behind the one-way glass and tell me that my old friend is not, in fact, drunk and crazy and no thanks to me out on the street now. The traveler was for real. Those footsteps I hear on the porch might well be hers—and she might be really pissed off now. Even if I never see her again, she's a young woman in deep trouble. She asked me for help, and I couldn't help her. And she was once my friend. Just when I need positive emotions to restore my good health, there seems very little to smile about. I don't want to go out with friends, I don't want to do creative work, I don't notice beautiful things in the gutter. My dilemma harks back to the inner conflict so many women expressed when I first interviewed them about happiness. "How can we be happy when so many people in the world are suffering?" Any attempt to cheer myself up seemed almost in poor taste. Still, what good was my anxiety doing anyone?

A few days after I chased the traveler out, I got a text message from a massage student offering me a free treatment. I could certainly use it, so I accepted. According to Fredrickson, two distinct positive emotions—mild joy and contentment—share the ability to kick the undo effect into action. Even if I couldn't laugh at my recent experiences, maybe I could conjure up a little bit of contentment. After all, it's hard to be grumpy when you're getting a free massage.

As the student manipulated my muscles, I thought about everything I was stressed-out about, and then, slowly, I started to let it go. I spaced out. I thought of nothing much. I thought of the sidewalk outside my house. I pictured the slick shine of the rain-wet streets. I thought about ways to block the hole in the corner of my attic so the squirrels couldn't get inside anymore. In my mind's eye, I saw expanses of water, blue-green, reflecting shards of sunlight. Under a steely autumn sky, I imagined the traveler finding her way in this world, and I sent up a little psychic vote for the best outcome. I thought of all the other crazy people I'd known in my life, and it occurred to me that this one had come to teach me about boundaries and the limits of hospitality. In my ideal book of ethics, no one seeking food or shelter should ever be turned away. In real life, there are limits. The night before I chased her out, the traveler looked me squarely in the eyes for a split second and slurred, "You're my mother." In *Women Who Run with the Wolves*, Clarissa Pinkola Estés points out that fairy tales often begin with the death of a sweet and protective mother because there comes a time in all our lives when the too-good mother has to die. So I entertained the possibility that the traveler had come to me to learn something, too. At the very least, I could acknowledge that at this point in her journey, the last thing she needed was the enabling mother figure she saw in me. Allowing her to feed her insanity with wine in my kitchen wasn't helping her. So out she went.

By the time my massage was over, I'd reimagined both of our lives into stories that didn't end tragically, and I sent up another psychic vote for complex and soulful happy endings.

I've taught a memoir-writing workshop for the past eight years, and if I've learned anything from my students, it's that the act of writing our lives has an intrinsically healing effect. Students don't come to my workshops for therapy, but by telling their stories, they begin to see their experiences—especially their negative experiences—as part of a longer life narrative. When we can see the big picture, and begin to understand some part of the vast context in which things happen, that seeing eases the resonance of whatever it is that haunts us.

I once remarked to a chronically depressed friend that life has an intrinsic elegance we can trust.

She thought about that for a few minutes. "See," she finally said. "I don't believe that."

Literature on depression has documented a downward spiral in which a bum mood and a pessimistic outlook feed each other, leading to an ever-worsening state of mind. The broaden-and-build theory points to a complementary upward spiral in which contentment and joy, and the broad thinking those emotions bring about, also feed each other, leading to greater resilience and an ever-rising capacity for inspiration.

We can put the undo effect to use by meeting our experiences with good humor, by actively seeking positive emotional experiences on the heels of our stress-fests, or, at the very least, by allowing ourselves time to relax and imagine how our crappy days might fit into a larger, less crappy context.

As Fredrickson says, we should cultivate positive emotions not just because we like them but also because doing so transforms us for the better and sets us on our paths toward flourishing and healthy longevity.

I mean, guess which one of these nuns lived longer.

Was it Sister No. 1, who wrote, "I was born on September 26, 1909, the eldest of seven children, five girls and two boys . . . My candidate year was spent in the Motherhouse, teaching Chemistry and Second Year Latin at Notre Dame Institute. With God's grace, I intend to do my best for our Order, for the spread of religion and for my personal sanctification"?

Or was it Sister No. 2, who wrote, "God started my life off well by bestowing upon me a grace of inestimable value . . . The past year which I have spent as a candidate studying at Notre Dame College has been a very happy one. Now I look forward with eager joy to receiving the Holy Habit of Our Lady and to a life of union with Love Divine"?

Yes indeed, Sister No. 2 got a full decade longer for her union with the Love Divine. If you're going to be a nun, after all, you might as well not be a grumpy nun.

when the smiley scientists meet

When Marion Milner set out to keep her happiness diary at age twenty-six, her first entry was hardly inspirational: "Rather oppressed with the number of things that need to be done." I feel rather oppressed myself.

—FROM ARIEL'S JOURNAL

When the alarm goes off at 4:00 a.m., I'm already awake and nursing the baby. I crawl out of bed, hold him with one arm, and use the other to gather all the clothes and diapers and notebooks and articles I meant to pack last night. Maria makes a pot of thick black coffee and does a last-minute load of laundry. As we drag onto the plane a couple of hours later, the passengers in the seats around us stare in held-breath dread. They obviously got up earlier than usual themselves, and I guess they hadn't planned on sharing the cross-country flight with a newborn. I want to apologize to each of them in advance, but I just offer a shy smile. I'm still trying to learn optimism.

As the plane takes off, I send up a thin prayer, and—*hallelujah*—baby Max yawns and snuggles into sleep. He's six weeks old, this baby of mine. He can wail like some pained bird, but now he just wakes to eat or look around our aisle, wide-eyed and silent. I kiss his soft head, decide it was a good idea to have him. *Quite a good idea.* He grins, Buddha boy. He isn't even fazed when a jubilant stewardess gets right up in his face and squeals as she offers him a "First Flight" certificate. The passengers around us all smile when we snap his picture. They're afraid to compliment him on his calm, of course, for fear that they'll jinx it. They wait until the plane is safely at its arrival gate before they exhale. "Your baby is *so* good," they coo.

A bus ride and a subway trip later, and we're finally in balmy Washington, D.C. We check into an old hotel a few blocks from the White House. Sadly, the guests in the rooms around us aren't as lucky as our fellow travelers on the plane. The baby wakes every hour to exercise his lungs. He eats, falls back asleep, wakes again too soon. When the alarm clock sounds again, I feel like the subject of some twisted psychological experiment. I rub my eyes. *What on earth are we doing here?*

We've traveled all this way to find out what researchers are saying about the optimal conditions for cultivating happiness.

While I've been reading up on the history of cheerfulness and depression, recording moments of contentment, interviewing hundreds of women, and ushering this new life into the world, scientists have spent another busy year doing what scientists do best—coming up with hypotheses, conducting experiments, gathering evidence, proving theories, and preparing their presentations for the ninth annual Positive Psychology Summit. I try not to dwell on the irony that I've been suffering from periodic bouts of weeping. I write off my depressive symptoms to old-fashioned baby blues—perhaps the result of plummeting estrogen levels and the hard-candy knowledge that the world will soon disappoint my sweet, milk-faced boy.

As the sun rises outside our hotel window, I pump breast milk and read two new studies that trace a growing gender gap when it comes to happiness. In one study, University of Pennsylvania economists looked at traditional happiness data in which people were asked how happy they felt with their overall lives as well as how they felt about specific aspects of life, like their marital status or marriage, their health, and their work. Thirty-five years ago, women reported being slightly happier than men. Today, we've switched places. The gender gap isn't huge, but it's statistically significant, and it shows up in every age-group from adolescence through retirement. The biggest drop in subjective well-being has been recorded among women my own age— those of us in our thirties and early forties.

In the second study, a Princeton economist and a group of psychologists looked at time-use data and found an even starker reality. Since the 1960s, men have gradually cut back on activities they found unpleasant—they now work less and relax more. Over the same time span, women have replaced housework with paid work, but we still do a larger share of child-rearing, cooking, cleaning, and elder care. Adding alienation to overwork, women now spend less time with friends and more time watching television.

Both studies show an absolute decline in happiness among women and an even steeper decline in women's happiness relative to men's.

As I head over to the Gallup Building for the Positive Psychology Summit, I try to wrap my mind around the new studies. Would researchers find the same decline in happiness among the women I know? Are we, in fact, less happy than our mothers were? Since I was a kid, the wage gap between women and men has narrowed. We are now more likely than our brothers to go to college. We've gained significant control over our reproductive lives. And nobody really cares if we don't dust the bookshelves. Individual studies show that women's life satisfaction increases with each of these changes. So what's the deal? The study authors were careful not to bash feminism, but they did suggest ways in which the women's movement may have failed us.

Interestingly, few psychologists mention set-point theories when they talk about women's improved lot in life. Perhaps second-wave feminism was the equivalent of winning the lottery for women. If so, the change up and the promise of more might have been the most thrilling part. Now that we've gotten used to our paychecks and our IUDs, maybe we've just set our sights on new goals. And maybe this time we're not so confident that we're going to make the same progress. The 1970s were a time of great momentum and greater hope. Perhaps our mothers were happy, in part, because they knew their children's lives would be better than their own. I revel in the freedoms I do have, but I'm not so sure what the future holds for my kids. Sometimes the view forward is as important as the ground we stand on.

I duck into a coffee shop.

Between the jet lag and the baby, I can't remember ever being so tired. I order a double latte and can't help but notice the two other people getting caffeinated at this hour: a woman who simultaneously marks up a spreadsheet and coordinates children's schedules on her cell phone, and a man who taps his foot to an iPod tune as he sips his mocha. *It's all so cliché.*

When I finally step inside the marble-floored Gallup Building ten minutes later, I wonder how many of these people got up at dawn to pump milk before the morning events. As I survey the crowd, I think, for some reason, of a Kenneth Patchen poem called "Because Everybody Looked So Friendly I Ran." But I do not run. I take a deep belly breath. I recognize a lot of the folks here from their author photos. Martin Seligman and Jonathan Haidt, Mihaly Csikszentmihalyi and Ed Diener—these are the stars of the new happiness science. I'm surprised to see just as many women in the crowd as men, but I don't recognize any of them. After I pile my breakfast plate with fruit and toast and eavesdrop on a dozen conversations, I begin to understand that here, as in so many of the healing professions, the practitioners tend to be female—in this case, the life coaches and the counselors—but the "experts" and authors are predominantly male. Still, in just the few years since I've been paying attention, the number of women in the field has begun to climb. "Don't blame positive psychology for being male dominated," one female academic has already warned me. "Negative psychology is even worse."

Perhaps more important, Sonja Lyubomirsky has assured me, when it comes to intentional strategies for cultivating happiness, "we've looked but have never found gender differences. That is, women don't obtain greater or less benefit from the strategies we've tested than do men."

Still, after one of the first panel discussions of the morning, a female psychologist in the audience stands up, mentions the growing happiness gender gap, and asks the all-male group onstage why the positive psychology movement has ignored women's issues. She is quickly silenced. One doctor denies that anyone is ignoring women, another denies that there is any gender gap, and a third insists that there's no difference between men and women anyway.

Their answers are unsatisfying, but I'm not here to bang my head against the wall. On to what I've come to find out about—the optimal conditions for cultivating happiness, intentional strategies and all. Lyubomirsky has told me that if I want to be happier, I ought to put gratitude and kindness at the top of my to-do list. "Thanks," I say, smiling, and I shuffle off to listen to presentations on the latest findings about being grateful. As the morning eases on, I learn about the other staples of positive psychology, like meditation, focusing on our strengths rather than our neuroses, and choosing to spend our resources on positive experiences rather than on material things. These are proven and uncontroversial strategies for boosting our mood without psychotropic drugs, but other ideas are up for debate. Can money buy happiness? Conventional wisdom in the field has held that income and happiness go hand in hand only until our basic needs are met. Once we're out of poverty's reach—about thirty thousand or forty thousand dollars a year for a small U.S. household—more money does little to increase our happiness. The new Gallup World Poll, however, shows a stronger than expected correlation between a nation's average income and the population's sense of well-being. "We might have to take another look at materialism," says the renowned psychologist Ed Diener.

Nic Marks, founder of the New Economics Foundation's Centre for Well-Being in London, disagrees. "Materialism isn't what's making us happy," he says. "Materialism is destroying the planet." He finds fault with some of the Gallup World Poll's questions in which respondents were asked to imagine an ideal life. "More people have access to television than to running water," he reminds us. Because they are exposed to media images of privilege and mass consumption, "it's not surprising that people feel badly about themselves." The New Economics Foundation's "(Un)Happy Planet Index" combines environmental impact with human well-being data to measure the environmental efficiency with which, country by country, people lead long and happy lives. The idea is that if the population of a country like Bhutan or Colombia can achieve an average happiness rating of, say, 7.5 on a scale of 1 to 10 while using only its relative share of the world's natural resources, they're a lot better off than a country like the United States, where the population enjoys only the same level of well-being but uses more than nine times its share of resources—leaving a giant carbon footprint with no added benefit for its people. "The future needs to be happier, fairer, and lower carbon," Marks says.

At lunchtime, I sneak off to take the New Economics Foundation's online survey to measure my own "Personal Happy Planet Index." I discover that I'm similar to someone living in western Europe: I'm happier than most people in the world, but I'm using four times my share of the earth's resources. *Ouch.* Better than the average American, but not particularly efficient. I also learn that—lucky for me, but maybe not so lucky for the planet—I can expect to live well into my eighties. I vow to decrease my carbon footprint, then rush out to meet Maria and feed the baby on the steps of the National Museum of American History. I'm back at the summit in time to pick up a bagged lunch, but before I can grab a bottle of water, I'm cornered by a couple of life coaches who want to know why I seem rushed. "You can savor this moment now," one of them reminds me. Her purple eye shadow is heavier on one side than the other.

My morning nervousness returns, a flutter behind my heart. I don't like to think that I'm uncomfortable around cheerful people, but there's something of a missionary vibe here that seems odd for a professional conference. I smile and nod, take a step back to signal my disinterest in the conversation, but these two have more insights they want to share with me.

"I've learned to simply stop and center," the other woman tells me. She has a short blond pageboy. She points to the middle of her forehead with her index finger and traces a line down her middle, stopping at her belly button. "Center," she says again, as if perhaps I'm not very bright.

The weird thing is that I don't feel terribly rushed or uncentered. "Thanks," I say. "I think I'm okay."

Purple eye shadow cocks her head to the side. "No one ever says, 'I want to be okay when I grow up,' now, do they?"

I'm starting to feel kind of panicky—I just want to eat my roasted veggie sandwich and drink my little bottle of water—so I blurt the first thing that comes to mind: "Oh my gosh—look!" I point. "There's Martin Seligman!" As my life coaches turn, I make a quick escape.

The enigmatic Martin Seligman remains at the edge of the crowd, where he's been all day, looking mildly grumpy. He's usually deep in conversation with a colleague or a student, another hovering nearby. I've heard him referred to here as a godfather, a guru, as simply "Marty." In a workshop on social change, the presenter projected a famous image of Gandhi—but with Marty's face pasted over Mahatma's. If positive psychology were a religion, I think, Marty would surely be its living saint.

When the good doctor finally takes the stage in the Great Hall here at the Gallup Building, I imagine he's going to summarize the latest studies and suggest ideas for future research. I settle into my seat behind several hundred others to listen and take notes. But Marty has bolder talking points on his agenda. To audible gasps and almost immediate controversy, he drops a positive psychology bombshell. "I've decided that my theory of positive psychology was completely wrong," he announces.

In his book *Authentic Happiness*, Seligman argued that there were three forms of happiness. He called them "the pleasant life," "the engaged life," and "the meaningful life."

The pleasant life consists in having as many pleasures as possible and having the skills—the timing, the ability to savor, and the mindfulness—to make the most of those pleasures instead of spinning off into some endless and exhausting ecstasy rave. The engaged life has more to do with what's called "flow," with being energized and so completely absorbed in whatever we're doing that time seems to lose its relevance. The meaningful life, finally, is about working for something bigger than ourselves so at day's end we can say, *I did what I could and I deserve a beer.*

"That's not it at all," Seligman says now.

For some reason, this makes me happy. I do like a philosophical curveball. I realize that my discomfort here at the summit has had a lot to do with the fact that positive psychology sometimes feels more like a religion than a science. To contradict Martin Seligman—even to suggest that he doesn't have all the answers—has felt like something akin to heresy, but now that he's contradicted himself, all the positive psychologists are in a tizzy. They're red-faced and confused. They're muttering to themselves and to each other. And then they start arguing with Seligman. As the fight gets under way, I begin to relax. Marty is highly respected here, but it's nice to see that he isn't a god.

As the dust settles, it occurs to me that Seligman's new theory isn't a huge departure from his old theory. Despite his provocative declaration, a careful listen reveals that he's simply expanded his conception of the good life, adding two new forms of happiness to his list—positive relationships and accomplishment.

I'm excited about this first addition because it promises a feminization of positive psychology—or at least a move closer to relational psychology. Responsibility to relationship, as Carol Gilligan and other psychologists have shown, is a primary motivator when it comes to women's decision-making and moral development.

It's the next one—accomplishment, the fifth form of happiness—that really has the smiley scientists in an uproar. An avid bridge player, Seligman explains it this way: Some people play bridge because they find it pleasurable, some play it because they find it engaging, some play because they find it meaningful, some play for the social network, and, well, some people cheat. They just want to win. They pursue accomplishment in and of itself.

Jonathan Haidt, author of *The Happiness Hypothesis*, stands up immediately and argues that there are traps when it comes to happiness and maybe accomplishment without virtue is just a trap. I wondered whether separate studies would find a gender difference here—surely there are differences in how men and women have been taught to understand achievement and its worth. The subtle differences in our moral development would certainly come into play.

Someone comments that the pursuit of accomplishment without the thrill of victory might be akin to learned helplessness, and pretty soon the whole crowd is a-chatter with academic arguments about morality, science, and the makings of a life worth living. I can feel my milk letting down. The baby is hungry, so I gather my notebooks and sneak out, leaving the positive psychologists to their new conundrum.

I'm already thinking about the next day's presentations. For today, I'm pleased with my list of happiness boosters:

Gratitude
Kindness
Meditation
Learning to focus on our strengths rather than on our shortcomings
Money/resources to keep us out of poverty's reach
Positive relationships

Clearly Seligman is onto something when he talks about accomplishment, too, but his detractors have a point. The cheating example might not quite fit. Nobody likes a cheater. But that's probably a topic for next year's summit—surely someone is already at work designing a study to find out whether or not cheaters like themselves. Accomplishment might make us happy, but if we are concerned with morality, too, cheating might leave us feeling more conflicted—perhaps pleased at what we appear to have done and, at the same time, empty and self-loathing because we know we're liars. If our moral compass points to responsibility to relationship, we're going to have a pretty hard time if our accomplishments come at the expense of others.

I head back to the hotel, and in the morning I do it all again. I sit through presentations fascinating and dull and add a couple more optimal conditions to my list:

Inspiration
Flow
Accomplishment (preferably without cheating)

One of the last sessions on the last day of the summit promises to be just what I've come all this way for—the latest findings on "well-being, emotional life, and gender." And so I've waited. But in the brief and singularly unenlightening presentation I learn . . . exactly . . . nothing.

The presenter mumbles, barely intelligible. He seems at once miserable and oddly intimidated by the whole scene. Maybe he has jet lag. Or maybe he's staying in the same hotel as I am and my baby kept him up all night. But it occurs to me that he doesn't seem to think he's important enough to be here. I squint at his slides and move closer to try to hear him. It's no use. He's just begun, and already he's wrapping it up. A presentation that was supposed to go on for at least twenty minutes is over in five. I remember an interesting tidbit at the end of Tal Ben-Shahar's book *The Question of Happiness*. He brings up the concept of "metaphysical worthiness" as a prerequisite for a happy life. How can we enjoy ourselves if we don't think we deserve to enjoy ourselves? How happy can we be if we feel as if we have to apologize for the fact that we're even here? Because of our conditioning, our experience of discrimination and abuse, and the particular way in which products are marketed to us, women often have an even harder time when it comes to remembering our intrinsic worth. Our inner nurturers might be beautifully developed, but that development doesn't always include the sense that we, too, deserve to be taken care of—that we have a right and a responsibility to take care of ourselves. "I think we are intrinsically maternal beings," Calliope said at our liberation psychology forum. "And we like to be mothered. I think we like caring for and being cared for. Happiness comes when we are balanced in both roles." We can only find that balance when we feel equally worthy of each. Before I put my list away, I add:

Metaphysical worthiness

I gather up my papers and head out. Even though some of the presentations were disappointing, I'm excited. "Just sitting in those little lecture halls, listening to people's ideas, taking notes. I love all that," I tell Maria when I get back to our little hotel room. "Listening to this one presentation, I just remembered how much I loved being in school. Just sitting around and thinking."

She tells me about all the free museums and galleries she took the baby through, the art and the inspiration. "I want to take a painting class when we get home," she says. "But for now I just want to take a nap."

I pick up my son and leave her to sleep, take the elevator downstairs to the sidewalk café. I feed the baby, order a pot of tea.

"How old is he?" my waitress wants to know.

"Six weeks."

"Name?"

"Maximilian."

She smiles at him. She's young, maybe twenty-two. She wears the same red uniform polo shirt as everyone else who works here, but hers is cropped to show off a belly-button ring. "You just have one baby?" she asks.

"I have a seventeen-year-old daughter as well."

The waitress lets her jaw drop dramatically. She sits down in the chair across from me and leans toward me as if we're old gossip buddies. "You don't look old enough to have a grown-up daughter," she whispers. She bites her lip as if she's about to tell me a secret. "I have a four-year-old," she says.

"If you're old enough to have a four-year-old, I'm old enough to have a teenager."

She thinks about that, nods. "I just want another baby," she says. "My daughter makes me so happy." Another waitress passes our table, and mine reaches out to her, tugs at her shirt. "Isn't her baby beautiful?"

The other waitress smiles down at him. "He's super-cute," she says.

"Don't you just *want* a baby?" my new waitress friend asks her coworker.

The other young woman shakes her head. "No offense," she says. "But I thank God every day for birth control."

"No offense taken," I assure her.

She glances back at my waitress. "Aren't you supposed to be working?"

"I guess so." The young mother stands up and shrugs. A few minutes later, she brings me my tea, gazes at Max again, and shakes her head.

I get out my list and add:

Motherhood—or not (self-determination)

THE FOURTH QUESTION
*Do you think you're happier or less happy
than your mother was at your age?*

⁜

I asked a hundred women, "Do you think you're happier or less happy than your mother was at your age?" Their responses stood in stark contrast to the recent studies that have found a decline in women's well-being over the past thirty-five years. Instead of carefree housewives, daughters described mothers who had lost themselves in child-rearing, in marriages, in low-wage labor. The median age difference between the daughters I asked and their mothers was just under thirty years, but more than 75 percent of the daughters I asked judged themselves to be happier than their mothers. The other 25 percent were split evenly between those who believed their mothers were happier and those who thought it was a toss-up. Asking a daughter to recall her mother's happiness is a far cry from asking both mothers and non-mothers how they feel about their lives, but these answers suggest some interesting questions about why researchers may have been able to trace that decline in happiness. What is it that truly makes us happy? Are we reliable judges of our own happiness? Why might we say we were happy if we weren't?

I'm happier. I have a community that's willing to help me, the time and energy to pursue my own interests and not get sucked into the workaday grind, friends who love and cherish me, and people who are willing to help me when I need it.

I think I'm happier than my mother was—I have more friends, stronger relationships, and fewer addictions.

I think in some ways I'm less satisfied than my mother was at my age—mostly because she didn't analyze things quite as incessantly as I do. I suspect that was partly a product of the times and partly due to her upbringing. I have always envied her ability to just roll with life and accept the things she's chosen.

About the same, but for different reasons. My mom was pleased with her family and material wealth at thirty-one. I am pleased as well with my family (meaning my friends), but I'm more satisfied with my spiritual life. That aspect didn't really emerge in my mother's life until she was in her forties.

I'd say I'm happier and more satisfied. The proof? I don't yell at people or have high blood pressure. The funny thing is, I think my mother would have said she was happy, pointing to things she was proud of, like a thirty-year marriage, her religion, and two cars in the driveway.

I think I'm more fulfilled than Mom was at this age. I'm forty-six. I have more choices, and I live in a society that supports my choices—from the availability of child care to the family-friendly atmosphere and policies I enjoy at work. I have twenty immediate family members in the area who are helping me to raise my child. At forty-six, my mom was in a bad marriage, she hated her job, and was almost done raising seven kids.

Happier. My mother worked a lot and her body hurt. She was short on money and time. She struggled to integrate a mental-health diagnosis for which she took prescription drugs. She had five demanding humans dependent on her for their food and affection and support—and we didn't give much back.

I think I am more authentically happy at this age. When my mother was my age, she had the things that she was "supposed" to have—two children and a husband—but she was deeply unhappy and unsatisfied with her choice of a husband and the life he was giving her. He was in the military and was pretty cold and distant. It seems like she spent the rest of her life trying to find independence and what it was that she loved to do. On the other hand, I am doing the opposite of what I'm "supposed" to be doing. I'm a single lesbian living alone in a city away from my family and trying to live through art. Even though it seems more stressful to me day to day, I'm doing work that I love and building a life made up of my childhood interests.

Happier. I feel free and independent and inspired all the time.

I'm much happier than my mom. She stayed married to a tyrant with whom she had nine kids by the time she was thirty-six. She had no freedom and was agoraphobic. She would claim she's happy, and I won't deny her that, but I have so much more freedom. I've traveled halfway around the world; I've twice had the pleasure of divorcing men who treated me like shit—an option she never had because of her generation, beliefs, and religion. We haven't had enough changes in society, but at least I was able to make a living, have and raise a kid, and buy a house without having to have a man involved in those processes.

I think I'm way happier than my mom was. She was already saddled with two kids she didn't want, she hated her parents, hated her husband,

and had given up on most of her dreams. At this point, she was hating her life.

I'm happier and more satisfied. At my age, my mother was in a struggling marriage, living an isolated life in a tiny Ohio town, with a seven-year-old son and a husband who worked constantly. I'm in a very happy, stable relationship. I have two kids who make me happy, and I'm finishing up my college degree, which I thought I might never get around to doing. We struggle to make ends meet, but I sometimes find myself looking around my home and thinking, Wow. I'm happy. Who would have figured? *I spent years being a very unhappy person, so sometimes being so fundamentally satisfied still feels very new—I can't get used to it.*

if you're hokey and you know it, clap your hands

✻

Interesting that my knee-jerk reaction is to want to write about my discomforts and grievances.

—FROM LINDA'S JOURNAL

At home and in the light of morning, I study my list of ideas and strategies for cultivating well-being. I decide to start with what looks to be the easiest: cultivating gratitude. When scientists began examining the links between religion and good health, a few soon narrowed their focus in on the relationship between gratitude and happiness. Religious people had better mental health and scored higher when it came to happiness, they decided, in part because the world's major religions all prize gratitude. To make matters even simpler, researchers soon found that gratitude could function independent of religion. Study after study proved the gratitude theory. All I had to do was express my thanks in a journal every day for six weeks. I'd acknowledge the goodness in my life and recognize that some of that goodness came from outside of myself. In doing so, I could increase my happiness and decrease depressive symptoms in as little as three weeks.

What's not to like about that?

A gratitude journal—*cheap and easy.*

I chose a simple blank book with lined pages and put it in the drawer of my nightstand. Every evening before I went to bed, I'd list a few things I felt thankful for.

Taking up the gratitude practice did turn out to be cheap, but, alas, nothing is ever quite as easy as it sounds.

At first, writing the entries feels kind of hokey:

I am thankful for the Pacific Ocean.
I am thankful for Lucinda Williams.
I am thankful for Ana Helena's Colombian stew . . .

I mean, I do feel grateful. For the ocean and for music and for that tasty chicken and plantain stew. I thank the stars daily for my children's good health, for the work I'm overwhelmed with, for my warm little house near the rail yard, for the ginger soda and spicy tuna rolls at Sushi Ichiban. But when it comes time to put my appreciation into words, something inside of me contracts. I feel like a freckle-faced little kid. I can't help but think of the childhood "thank-you notes" I was forced to write every time I opened a gift. On pink Hello Kitty stationery, I expressed my glee over Christmas and birthday presents I may or may not have liked. I remember receiving those notes, too, and understanding that they were formalities exchanged between family members—they meant nothing.

Did my red Cadillac maternal grandmother really think the dime-store perfume I'd given her was "simply marvelous"? She certainly sent the "thank you" promptly enough. On her Museum of Modern Art note card, she raved poetic about my choice of scents.

Looking back, I'm sure she appreciated the fact that I'd sent her a gift, but she couldn't have liked the perfume itself. My grandmother wouldn't have dreamed of dabbing anything but Coco Chanel or Paloma Picasso behind her ears.

I liked it when my grandmother sent me gifts, too, but my sister and I often exchanged a smirk and mumbled "It's the thought that counts" as we unfurled yet another unwearable wool sweater. We laughed, but we meant it about the thought. We did appreciate it. We knew that the unwearable wool sweater was our grandmother's way of expressing her love to us, and we welcomed her love. Still, we had to write the thank-you note for the *sweater*.

And so it happens that when I settle into bed on the third night of my gratitude experiment and open my black journal, ready to count my blessings, I instead find myself processing my bad relationship with gratitude.

Dear Gammie,
Thank you for the Holly Hobbie oven. It was the only thing I really wanted for Christmas. I begged you for it because I wanted to be as cool as Michelle Carson and bake little chocolate chip muffins in it. I dreamed of giving those little muffins to Michelle and all the other girls in the club I started—the one they voted me out of a few weeks later because they said they didn't want anyone in their club with curly hair. I just knew that if I got a Holly Hobbie oven like Michelle, the straight-haired girls would call a special meeting and they'd vote me back in. Anyway, Gammie, it's okay that you got the wrong oven and that this one doesn't cook anything at all. What I wanted was a Holly Hobbie Bake Oven like the one Michelle has, and this is just a big metal play oven that happens to have little pictures of Holly Hobbie on the sides. This one is for little kids, not for fourth graders like me, and I think it's supposed to go inside a playhouse with other Holly Hobbie things, but I don't have a playhouse, and now with this big metal oven in my

room I'll never be able to invite Michelle or any of the other
straight-haired girls over again. But, like I said, Gammie, thank
you. I know you wanted to get me what I wanted, and that means
a lot to me. Maybe I can come and visit you soon and we can go to
the beach and I can forget about Michelle and all the straight-
haired girls and we can sit in your special beach chairs on the shore
and eat pickle sandwiches and watch the tide come in.

Much love,
Ariel

I'm not alone in my conflict. In a 1998 Gallup poll, a majority of Americans said they expressed gratitude "all the time," but
according to Robert Emmons, editor of *The Journal of Positive
Psychology* and an expert on the psychology of gratitude, we
actually talk about being thankful pretty infrequently. Anger,
resentment, and romantic love get all the talk time—not to
mention all the radio play. It occurs to me that we're such a
nation of ingrates that our language of appreciation hasn't
evolved beyond those forced childhood thank-you notes.

"Gratitude presupposes so many judgments about debt and
dependency that it is easy to see why supposedly self-reliant
Americans would feel queasy about even discussing it," Emmons
says. "We like to think that we are our own creators and that our
lives are ours to do with as we please. We take things for granted.
We assume that we are totally responsible for all the good that
comes our way. After all, we have earned it. We deserve it."

It's like Bart Simpson puts it when he's asked to say grace at
the family dinner table: "Dear God, we paid for all this stuff ourselves, so thanks for nothing."

Speaking of the dinner table, let's not forget Thanksgiving. If
all those inauthentic thank-you notes weren't enough to make
me feel weird about genuine gratitude, the annual celebration

probably would have done the trick. Every year, after the leaves have fallen from the trees, on the fourth Thursday in November, we spend the afternoon commemorating indigenous peoples' generosity in the face of white settlers' aggression.

When I open my gratitude journal on the seventh night of my experiment, it occurs to me that I might rather settle into bed with an *ingratitude* journal. It's making me feel bad that this gratitude thing doesn't come naturally to me. I feel like an ingrate. And the language of complaining seems so much more, well, satisfying. I could write about what a bitch that one positive psychologist I had to interview was and how I just *knew* she was jealous of my book contract.

Okay, so maybe my language of complaining isn't exactly the model of maturity.

I force myself to continue. People who practice gratitude regularly can increase their set point for happiness by as much as 25 percent, I reminded myself. In as little as three weeks I might be sleeping better, have more energy, and feel more connected to my friends and community.

> *I'm thankful that Lisa came over to watch the baby so I could write my chapter.*
>
> *I was too tired to cook tonight and I just wanted some yummy comfort food, so, even though I couldn't afford it, we went out to get dinner at SubRosa and—randomly—just because of the baby—the owner said dinner was on the house. She even gave us a pizza to take home.*
>
> *I'm grateful that I'm not as crazy as the guy I can hear ranting outside in the street right now.*

I put my gratitude journal in its drawer and lie back on my soft pillow, but I can't sleep. I creep out into the dark of the living room and turn on the TV. It's all commercials. A young career woman struts across a city street, smiling at what a great shade of lipstick she has on. *If I were that tall and thin*, I think, *I could really be happy*. Next, an older woman who has fewer wrinkles than I do relaxes in the desert sun, enjoying the fruits of her wise mutual fund investments. *It would be so great to be rich*, I think. Then a harried thirtysomething mom takes the screen. She's thin, and she appears to be rich, but she contorts her face into a caricature of mom stress. But then—magically—an animated giant appears in her kitchen and everything sparkles and the woman relaxes and she smiles, happy. I sigh. *If only I had a body like my teenage daughter, a bank account like my octogenarian grandmother, and a kitchen like the crazy lady on TV, I could be deeply and truly happy.* I grab the remote and switch the thing off, sit in the dark of my living room. I wonder how many ads I see in a given week. I switch on my laptop and ask Google. The average American, according to the *Consumer Reports* website, sees well over two hundred ads. And plenty of those are "product satisfaction" ads that teach us, again and again, to want the things we do not have. I slink back into my bedroom, look at the baby in his crib. He cries when he's hungry, wet, tired, or bored, but most of the time he gurgles and smiles, in love with all the goofiness of the world around him. No one has yet taught him that he should have a bigger house, brighter toys, cooler parents. I crawl into bed, close my eyes, and dream of all those things.

To assure myself that I'm not wasting my time with all this thankfulness, I spend my days reading studies about gratitude.

Children younger than seven don't always understand that gratitude means giving credit to others, I learn, but studies have found that older kids are relatively good at expressing their thanks. One study examined newspaper reports of what children said they were thankful for in the aftermath of 9/11. Kids expressed gratitude for friends and family as well as police, firefighters, and other helpers. Girls were generally more thankful than boys, and girls were more likely to mention the people and relationships in their lives. Boys were more likely to be grateful for material things.

In one "gratitude intervention" study at an upstate New York middle school, classes were randomly assigned to keep gratitude journals or chronicles of the hassles in their day-to-day lives. Over the course of two weeks, kids counted their blessings or their burdens. The blessings most often included caring and supporting relationships, good health, education, and sports. In the end, kids in the gratitude groups expressed more optimism and satisfaction with their lives.

In analyzing studies on kids, Emmons notes, "When we were children, we had no illusion of self-sufficiency. We were aware of our own dependence on our parents for survival, security, and comfort. As we grew, we were taught to look more and more to ourselves for the meeting of our needs. Eventually, we came to believe in the myth of our own self-sufficiency."

I roll those words around on my tongue. *The myth of self-sufficiency.*

I read on.

In studies of gratefulness in adults, women generally score higher than men. One study in the 1980s measured American, German, and Israeli attitudes toward emotional expression. Researchers found that Americans in general ranked gratitude relatively low in terms of its desirability and constructiveness.

American men, in particular, tended to view gratitude as unpleasant—even humiliating. Women found it much less difficult to express their thanks. Women, the study suggested, were more comfortable with their own dependence. That's when it struck me: *not this woman.*

I *felt* gratitude, but like the men in that 1980s study I ran into all kinds of resistance when it came time to *express* my gratitude. I may have felt comfortable with my dependence when I was a little girl, but I learned a fairly inauthentic language of "thank you," and that language never matured—not because I was ungrateful, but because the culture soon taught me that self-reliance meant strength. Anything else amounted to failure.

As a young mom, I was told both explicitly and implicitly that I wouldn't be able to take care of my daughter. My grandmother told me I needed a husband, acquaintances told me I needed to live with my parents, professors told me I'd never make it through college, politicians told me I'd always need welfare and they were "reforming" it. *You can't do it yourself*, folks said again and again. And they weren't offering me a hand. They were predicting my failure from the sidelines, arms folded and noses in the air, waiting to say, "I told you so."

But the stakes were too high for failure.

In the context of my single motherhood, I even grew wary of those who *did* offer me help. A relationship based on someone's idea that he or she was going to rescue me, I decided, was worse than no relationship at all. I wasn't a damsel in distress, thank you very much. And so, to protect myself and my small family, I developed an impeccable façade of self-sufficiency.

Far-out, I thought now. *I was just trying to make sure everybody understood I could take care of myself and my kid, and I ended up with this old-school American male aversion to expressing appreciation.* Not really what I was going for, but what could I do about it now?

I'd spent nearly eighteen years resisting dependence. I wasn't about to give in to the naysayers now. Instead, I printed out a little reminder and taped it to the cover of my little black gratitude journal:

I can take care of myself
AND
I can rely on others

Wow, I thought. *I am truly hokey.* I laughed, but my little affirmation seemed to work. As I soldiered on with my experiment, I read those words to myself, embraced my inner hokey-girl, and counted my blessings with growing ease. After about a month of gratitude journaling, I could see that the moments I noted in my happiness journal had become more frequent and more specific. The simple act of keeping notes on gratitude seemed to counter the misery engendered by consumerist culture and advertising in which we are taught to want what we do not have. With this simple nightly ritual, I was unraveling my own myth of self-sufficiency and training myself to want what I already had. It seemed to be working.

Gratitude. Hokey, perhaps. But what are we going to do? As the journalist Oliver Burkeman noted in *The Guardian*, "A terminal lack of coolness is, regrettably, endemic to happiness studies."

Clap your hands.

drudge and flow

❊

I was happy when I was writing, got lost in the writing. Adrienne Rich said, "Motherhood means being instantly interruptible, responsive, responsible." My friend Lynn says it's not just motherhood; it's womanhood. It's so rare now that I get lost in the writing, can allow myself the focus to lose track of time. I always have one ear tuned to the baby or to the jingle of the cell phone. Does everyone have what they need? What have I forgotten? In The Future Generation, *China Martens wrote, "I want to be the female Bukowski, the female Burroughs, but instead I'm just the female." I was happy when I forgot that I was just the female.*

—FROM ARIEL'S JOURNAL

I fold newspapers in the still-dark morning. I fold them in three and snap a rubber band around the middle. I am the first in our neighborhood to know that Mount St. Helens has erupted, that Ronald Reagan has won the presidency by a landslide, that John Lennon has been murdered. My fingers black with ink, I pack the newspapers into the metal basket of my sparkly blue three-speed bicycle. I pedal fast. I spread the news. As I approach each address on my route, I reach backward, grab a single newspaper, toss it onto a painted porch. If I pedal fast enough, I'm riding down Alma Street just as the freight train comes—a Southern

Pacific headed north toward San Francisco. I race the freight. I pedal faster and faster, but that train always wins. Sometimes when I'm running late, I don't catch sight or sound of the freight train at all. Maybe I've slept in, or maybe I've taken too long with the folding. I've pedaled too slow, or I've stopped to let some angry-sleepy customer yell at me about bad throws or bad news. The sun has crested the horizon. Now the train I hear is an Amtrak commuter barreling southward, bound for San Jose. I pedal faster. I have to finish my route. I am ten years old. I earn eighty dollars a month. I am the first in our neighborhood to know that Mount St. Helens has erupted, that Ronald Reagan has won the presidency by a landslide, that John Lennon has been murdered. I spread the news.

"That is happiness," Willa Cather wrote, "to be dissolved into something complete and great."

As my adolescence dawns, I will find other work. I will steam-iron designer blouses for $3.65 an hour, and I will burn my fingers, leaving scars smooth and white. I will serve sickly-sweet frozen yogurt to bone-thin women who ask, "How many calories per serving?" and throw it up in the bathroom. I will clean those bathrooms. I will count the hours. I will believe it when I learn that 80 percent of Americans hate their jobs. I will be those Americans. But I will remember my paper route and the way that the folding and the rubber-banding and the pedaling and the throwing felt like some divinely choreographed dance. I'll remember the way it felt to know that my work mattered, to believe it was something complete and great. I'll remember the dreamy stories I told myself even as I raced that Southern Pacific freight. I'll remember the taste of ink on my fingers. And even though I won't be able to fully imagine what I want to be when I grow up, I'll know I want work like that—work I can dissolve into like night into the dawn.

When we strike a balance between the challenge of an activity and our skill at performing it, when the rhythm of the work itself feels in sync with our pulse, when we know that what we're doing matters, we can get totally absorbed in our task. That is happiness.

The life coach Martha Beck asks new potential clients, "Is there anything you do regularly that makes you forget what time it is?"

That forgetting—that pure absorption—is what the psychologist Mihaly Csikszentmihalyi calls "flow" or optimal experience. In an interview with *Wired* magazine, he described flow as "being completely involved in an activity for its own sake. The ego falls away. Time flies. Every action, movement, and thought follows inevitably from the previous one, like playing jazz. Your whole being is involved, and you're using your skills to the utmost."

In a typical day that teeters between anxiety and boredom, flow experiences are those flashes of intense living—bright against the dull. These optimal experiences can happen when we're engaged in work paid and unpaid, in sports, in music, in art.

The researchers Maria Allison and Margaret Duncan have studied the role of flow in women's lives and looked at factors that contributed to what they call "antiflow." Antiflow was associated with repetitive household tasks, repetitive tasks at work, unchallenging tasks, and work we see as meaningless. But there's an element of chaos when it comes to flow. Even if we're doing meaningful and challenging work, that sense of total absorption can elude us. We might get completely and beautifully lost in something today, and, try as we might to re-create the same conditions tomorrow, our task might just feel like, well, work.

In *A Life of One's Own*, Marion Milner described her effort to re-create the conditions of her own recorded moments of happiness, saying, "Often when I felt certain that I had discovered the little mental act which produced the change I walked on air, exulting that I had found the key to my garden of delight and could slip through the door whenever I wished. But most often when I came again the place seemed different, the door overgrown with thorns and my key stuck in the lock. It was as if the first time I had said 'abracadabra' the door had opened, but the next time I must use a different word."

I felt the same way now as I looked back through the pages of my happiness journal. What was the variable that transformed experience from drudgery to engagement?

The women on my council of experts, too, recorded as happiest the experience of losing track of time or allowing themselves to be absorbed in work they thought of as meaningful and helpful. "I was happy seeing so many people involved in the clinic," Sonja wrote.

"I'm a teacher, and sometimes I just feel underpaid and unappreciated," one woman explained. "The kids are high-strung, and there are too many of them, and I get frustrated. You always hear about 'bad teachers,' but people have no idea how hard it is. But then sometimes something magical happens. It's like I get it in my head that the work I'm doing is important. All at once I'll catch my stride. The kids will catch their stride, too, and I'll see the genius in each of them and something will click and I'll be able to share my genius, too. It will all happen so quickly. Before I know it, the bell is ringing and it's over. But we could have stayed there for hours longer."

Like most Americans, we say we want more leisure time, but we're actually more likely to experience flow in the context of our work lives—work being anything that requires labor or results in the creation of a product, service, or experience, including paid and volunteer efforts, child-rearing, and creative action. Maybe it's because we're all so tired when we finally get to the weekend that we don't spend our "leisure" time reading or surfing or making music—activities in which it's easy to lose track of time in an expansive way—and instead zone out in front of the TV with a bowl of oversalted cheesy nachos.

When Utah Phillips launched his radio program, *Loafer's Glory: Hobo Jungle of the Mind*, I was a busy girl. It was the 1990s, and I was as ambitious as morning glory, wary of the do-nothing slackers in my life. But I was drawn to Phillips's show, drawn to the concept of a loafer's glory, drawn to Gertrude Stein's words as well: "It takes a heap of loafing to write a book." Here were two of the most productive artistic geniuses of the twentieth century—Gertrude Stein and Utah Phillips—slackers by no-body's standards, and they both championed the art and discipline of loafing, of idling the time away.

As I wrote books and raised my daughter through seasons harsh and bountiful, I began to understand that both endeavors did somehow take a heap of loafing, but I learned, too, that loafing is different from slacking. Loafing is an active, growing kind of time-out. Loafing knows nothing about stagnation. A loafer doesn't get stoned and watch TV every afternoon—that's what happens when we deny ourselves fair time to loaf until burnout and exhaustion take over and we collapse onto the couch. A loafer paints her toenails and waits for the polish to dry, steps out into the world, and wanders here and there, in nature or through bookstores, looking for nothing in particular. In lucid moments, I understood this time as necessary and delicious, but training myself to do nothing has been surprisingly difficult. I want to create, to produce. I need to make money. I refuse to be that mother who says to her children, "Sorry about the electricity, I am an artiste!" Or, "I really need to take care of my*self* right now."

Gertrude Stein was suggesting that we had to loaf in order to create, that it was not stagnant procrastination but part of the process, what makes us whole human beings on expansive journeys—and not rats in a wheel.

As I continued to meditate on my recorded moments of concentration, I noticed a few things that consistently blocked flow. Even worse than an activity being repetitive was the sense that I was interruptible. The fear of not having enough time to complete a goodly part of my task all but ruined any possibility that I might get lost in it. When I felt confident that I wouldn't be interrupted for a reasonable period of time, I could approach the door slowly and thereby have some chance of opening it. Worse, too, than a task being unchallenging was the sense that I was somehow being oppressed by it. When I felt that work was unfairly expected of me—when, for example, my daughter or my partner *expected* me to do what I considered more than my fair share—my bitterness ruined the experience. When I felt underpaid for commercial efforts, or when I had such financial anxiety that I couldn't imagine I had any choice in the focus of my labor, that sense of injustice precluded flow. Sometimes my entire workday—four to twelve hours—felt painstaking.

We have to step through all these blocks. As women, we have always been told what kind of work we ought to do—what kind of work we're fit for and what kind of work will make us happy. The family values campaign of the 1990s preached that middle-class mothers should stay home "for the sake of the children" while poor women should take "personal responsibility" and join the paid labor force. Middle-class and educated women were seen as dangerous competitors for high-paying male jobs and encouraged to jump onto a go-nowhere "mommy track." Corporate offices were glad to see us go. But the Walmarts of the world still needed cheap labor. Poor women got "welfare-to-work" programs and plenty of applications for low-paying jobs.

We need to be able to make true choices when it comes to our work lives. Even when we have to do work that feels like less than a "calling" or more than our fair share, we have to be able to find meaning and challenge therein.

Csikszentmihalyi and other researchers note that when study subjects are deprived of optimal experience in their day-to-day lives, they get tense and guarded, they report sleep problems, they feel weaker and more irritable, and they have shorter attention spans. And here I thought I was suffering from perpetual PMS.

In a recent presentation on the cost of flow deprivation in adolescence, Csikszentmihalyi pointed to alienation and even teenage violence as the direct results of the absence of flow. Not only do we enjoy flow experiences; it turns out we need them. Csikszentmihalyi admits that flow often occurs by chance, but he insists that we can consciously create all the conditions necessary for optimal experience.

The way he figures it, the components of flow are five-fold.

First, we have to be engaged in a challenging activity that requires skill. If we feel overqualified for our work, this can be tricky. It's why the repetitive tasks of housework are so difficult to transform into optimal experience. We play music to distract ourselves from the endless scrubbing, we arrange things according to complicated feng shui formulas to up the mental difficulty, or we challenge ourselves to turn the whole thing into some kind of high meditation. If we do none of these things, it's boring, and pretty soon boredom morphs into drudgery. If we're obligated to the drudge, we end up feeling oppressed and miserable. To make our work something we can stay interested in, we change the work itself, or by some intentional gesture of the mind we change our experience of it. We stop short of trying to do things that are way beyond our ability—that would just cause anxiety. We find the boundary between the two.

Second, we have to be able to allow ourselves the concentration to experience a merging of awareness and action. We have to be able to dedicate all our psychic energy to the task at hand. For a woman who is instantly interruptible, this seems to require an additional mental shift. Not to mention some boundaries. I work at home, so my family members are forever tempted to interrupt me.

"Can you just e-mail this attachment for me?"

"I know you're working, but can you print out this job description for me?"

"Do you know where the diaper bag is?"

And, "What's for dinner?"

There are days when I don't mind multitasking. I can do an amazing number of things at once. But there are times when I need focus, uninterrupted.

Even when my partner and kids can contain themselves, there is no end to the threat of interruption. We all have to find ways to be present and engaged in our work *despite* all the things that test our ability to concentrate. In the writing workshops I teach, most people turn off their cell phones, but a few—usually the single parents and the doctors—just switch their phones to a silent mode. They remain interruptible. The simple fact that the cell phone is on manages to distract some of those students from any meaningful engagement with the class. A necessary part of their mind is "on call" and therefore unavailable. Other students, I notice, seem unfazed by their interruptibility. Unless and until they're called away, they remain present. Anything *could* happen to any one of us. An earthquake or a blackout might interrupt even those who have no cell phone to silence. But some people seem to have mastered that little mental act by which they can quiet the mind-clamor that wastes so much of our time and energy worrying about an unpredictable future. If multiple roles are an intrinsic part of the modern female experience, we *have to* master that mental act.

The third component of flow clicks in when we have clear and achievable goals. Our activity has to give us some kind of immediate feedback on our progress. This is why sports and other games are designed the way they are—when we're playing tennis or running a marathon, we know what we have to do, and we know how much progress we've made. When our goals are more long-term—like rearing a child or growing a garden or earning a Ph.D.—we divide our task into shorter-term projects. We teach the child to read a word, we plant the carrot seeds, we write a paper on microeconomic theory and turn it in, hoping for an A.

The fourth necessity for flow is that we have to believe that we have some control over our experience. This is where the sense of oppression disrupts flow, and again where anxiety about all the bad things that might happen can get in our way. But even when we have limited control, we can learn to suspend our anxiety, to transform the oppressive circumstances, to focus on those small things we *do* have control over. Csikszentmihalyi has documented case after case when even prisoners were able to make games of their tasks and find flow in their work. Makes me feel kind of lame for being so annoyed about having to vacuum or only getting paid ten dollars an hour, but this isn't about accepting our exploitation—it's about facing the truth of our lives and finding freedom within the confines.

Finally, we have to be able to experience some reprieve from self-consciousness. Women described this reprieve again and again when I asked them to recall their happiest or most inspired moments. They talked about times when they felt one with a mountain trail, with a friend or a lover, with a project in the darkroom. They talked about making cartoons, working in a quiet office infused with sunshine, playing with a child at the beach. For a moment or an hour, they forget themselves. "Preoccupation with the self consumes psychic energy because in everyday life we often feel threatened," Csikszentmihalyi writes. "Whenever we are threatened we need to bring the image we have of ourselves back into awareness, so we can find out whether or not the threat is serious, and how we should meet it." He gives the example of walking down the street, noticing people grinning at him, and worrying about what he looks like or if something's wrong. Every woman alive knows this anxiety, this forced self-consciousness. Often our fear isn't just about whether or not we look funny—those looks and hollers can be more menacing. We're tired of being scrutinized, of being threatened. We are beyond tired of being the targets of intimidation, crime, and institutionalized violence on the streets, in our schools and hospitals, in our workplaces, and in our own homes.

It's no coincidence that my own most transcendent memories of flow are of childhood, of a time before I saw the world as threatening, and of the dawn hours, before those threats woke up. Still, sitting here at my computer, working on this chapter, immersed in the intimate communication that takes place between writer and reader, focusing on the rhythm of my words, the rhythm of my sentences, the rhythm of the computer keys, I hear a commuter train barreling down the nearby tracks, and I look up at the clock to see that the afternoon has gotten away from me. My phone is here. My children are out in the world. I am interruptible, but I have not been interrupted. And I feel the quiet contentment of my escape.

THE FIFTH QUESTION
What's the best thing that happened yesterday?

When I asked women to describe their fondest memory from the previous day, they focused on moments of solo inspiration and concentration, or on sweet interactions with friends, pets, children, or partners. We value our relationships. We value flow in our creative lives. We value the chance to get outside. We value everyday transcendent moments when we can finally forget ourselves.

Taking my dog to work with me. It's still dark when we leave the house, and she curls up in the passenger seat next to me. She's still kind of sleepy, and I scratch her ears while I'm driving.

At the campus café with friends, getting excited about who is taking which courses . . . it's registration time! Too many good classes, too many schedule conflicts.

Walking in the wilderness park with my dog and seeing the explosion of trilliums.

I was on the slopes, riding my snowboard on slushy snow, wearing a T-shirt because it was so warm, looking out at the surrounding mountains and the pine trees, feeling completely in love with my life.

Writing for uninterrupted hours in the reading room of Zimmerman Library at the University of New Mexico. The aesthetics of that room—high ceilings, Spanish-influenced furniture, massive adobe walls, and gorgeous natural light—are all conducive to creative thought. It's a luxury for me to have a full day to devote to writing. I'm still blissed-out.

Being in the darkroom and finally getting some good prints from my images of Hong Kong. I danced and swayed as I lifted each print from bath to bath while listening to Citizen Fish and the New Orleans Jazz Vipers and Gypsy bands, and I thought about burning a CD of music for my latest crush.

My husband called me and left a message just to tell me that he loved me.

Walking on this fabulous beach on an absolutely stunning day just as Alaska is beginning to think about spring. Breathtaking.

Watching my kids ride a rickety old go-kart down a muddy hill behind our house.

Looking on while my best friend told my daughter on the phone how to stand an egg on end because it was the vernal equinox. Between the two of them and the phone, they got that egg standing.

I sat watching my kids play in the playground and forgot myself for a few minutes.

I walked to dinner with my partner. The weather was mild and the light was gorgeous and there were lots of flowering trees. We were having an engaging conversation, and I knew we'd soon be eating good food.

In a move toward healing, my husband and I decided to go out to eat at the fanciest restaurant in town, using a gift certificate we received for our wedding. We parked on a street I had just been thinking about because that street is home to a heart-shaped pothole. We stood on the pothole and kissed.

Sitting at the hobo park after dark on the bluff overlooking Swan Island, watching the activity on the river and in the Union Pacific yard.

Staying up late to work on my comics after everyone else was asleep. It was quiet and still. I had some tea; the ideas were flowing.

E-mailing back and forth with my friend at midnight. She was telling me about this boy who was in town for a few days, who patched his pants with polka-dot material and wore a pink studded belt. He could speak three languages, and they were having a good time. She was preparing to have her first photography show—a show just for her! I was telling her about finishing my first book. We were both feeling very elated, that life is magic, and that we want it to be magic, and we are done with dull things that make us feel that life is limited.

extreme motherhood

✵

My kids take up so much of my time that sometimes I feel like "it's a busy time" or "all of this chaos will be over after _____ (fill in the blank)"—like the way you feel before a holiday. But then I wake up and realize that nothing is going to change. I'm going to be raising two kids for the next fifteen years. When I'm forty, I'm going to have a crisis and leave town; I'm sure of it.

—FROM BRITT'S JOURNAL

"I can't believe you decided to write a book about happiness when you were pregnant and postpartum," Maria says.

"I started the book before I got pregnant," I remind her, but she has a point.

Pregnancy is supposed to be one of the happiest times in a woman's life. In our cultural mythology, the birth of a child represents one of the doorways to "happily ever after." It's the moment, supposedly, that we've been putting off, settling down, and saving up for. But new motherhood is also associated with serious stress, with depression and intellectual demise. When Salon.com launched its parenting website, *Mothers Who Think,* back in the 1990s, there was plenty of controversy over the title. *Were the editors suggesting that some mothers didn't think?* Not exactly, but they were reacting to current media that seemed convinced that "like Pooh Bear, mothers are creatures of very little brains."

When I got pregnant at eighteen, so many of my feminist elders were aghast. *After all our work, this is what you choose? Single teenage motherhood?* As if having a child were akin to throwing my life away.

After my daughter was born, a lot of people we met assumed I was the nanny because of my age. I was good enough to care for her, but only as a member of the paid labor force.

When I got pregnant again at thirty-six, so many of my feminist elders were shocked—but only because it had been so long. No one questioned my ability, my life choice, my "future." Now I had a career, after all. Now I had a partner, a house, a car. Folks congratulated me on the "better circumstances" of this pregnancy, and I felt silently insulted. Suddenly I'd become the mother I'd always wondered about—the older mother, the partnered mother, the mother who had long since finished college and grad school. *Was she really more equipped?* I had always wondered. *Not really*, I'd soon learn. My second pregnancy was harder on my body than my first pregnancy, and the sleepless nights of early motherhood were harder on my spirit. It's nice to have a little bit more money, a house, and a car, but the baby doesn't seem to notice the difference. It's good to have a partner, too, but the future—all our futures—is an unknown. Most days, my life feels just as raw and complex as it did eighteen years ago.

When I got pregnant the first time, so many of my peers looked down their noses at me with an air of superiority. They planned to wait. They planned to marry. They planned to make big splashes with their careers. My life was over, they seemed to think.

When I got pregnant the second time, a few of my peers admitted they were jealous. They had waited. They had not married. They had not made such big splashes with their careers. They still had time, certainly, but they feared single motherhood like some bitter plague, and they felt even less "ready" than they had when we were young. Some friends had made the brave and decisive choice not to breed, but many more vacillated between fear and desire, their IUDs ticking the time out.

A few years ago, my grandmother told me a secret. "I look old," she said. She was eighty-five. "My body feels old," she said. "But a person's core never changes. At my core I'm the same as I was when I was eighteen."

Her words came as a surprise and a revelation. Would I never feel fully grown-up? Would I never feel "ready"?

Sometimes I think we're all just so afraid of life—of both youth and age. We're afraid of change, afraid to make choices, afraid to say, "This is the year." Sometimes I think we're all still afraid of how our feminist elders will react. We're waiting for a core change that doesn't come. We thought the years would bring a sense of security, a sense of clarity, but there is no year when a risk doesn't take courage.

Our ability to control our fertility is a beautiful thing—a crucial thing—but what if we don't really know what we want?

Over the course of our reproductive lives, most of us will be faced with the abortion decision. And over the course of our reproductive lives, most of us will have a child.

Six million women in America get pregnant each year. Half of our pregnancies are unplanned. Each year, about a million of us have abortions, about a million miscarry, and about four million give birth. Another two million undergo some kind of fertility treatment. And over 100,000 of us adopt a child. *Every single year.* By age forty-five, about half of all American women will have had at least one abortion, and about 80 percent of us will have at least one child. It all adds up to a great many years of our lives consumed in the hopes and fears and blood of birth and death.

If children don't come into our lives when we want them to or at all, we'll inevitably feel the pressure to explain ourselves. Those of us who know we want kids entertain conceptions about the "right" time and circumstances. We weigh our ideas of selfishness and responsibility. The scepter of "too late" waves at us from some preset age—thirty-six or forty-nine—and we scramble to meet the deadline or let go of desires fueled by our own longings as well as cultural and familial expectations. We are women, after all, and as suspiciously as they eye us for breeding too early, too late, or under questionable circumstances, they really give us the glare if we do not breed at all. "Barren," they call us. Or worse. At our liberation psychology forum, Jennifer told the story of taking her garbage out one evening and a neighbor telling her she ought to have her kids do the chore for her. She told him that she did not have any children.

"That's selfish," he barked.

"Don't you think it would be more selfish for me to have them and not do right by them?" Jennifer asked, even though her neighbor's comment hardly deserved a response. They just stared at each other then, across that driveway, split by gender and so much more, until Jennifer finally said, "Well, good night," and headed back inside.

There's little support for women who choose not to have children. But our communities hardly rally to help us if we do become moms.

A recent University of Iowa study found that low-income women were three times more likely to suffer from postpartum depression than wealthier women. We all have the same body chemistries, of course, so the study flies in the face of theories that blame only hormones.

In a second study, researchers found that black moms were more likely than white moms to be depressed, but that Latinas were *less* likely to be depressed. Think about that. The University of Iowa psychologist Lisa Segre explained it this way: "Research indicates that strong social support can serve as a buffer against postpartum depression, and that poor social support is a major predictor of postpartum depression. Past studies have also shown that Latina mothers tend to have more social support, while African American women tend to have weaker support net-works." Segre speculated that the ethnic differences in social support accounted for differences in our rates of postpartum depression.

If these studies hold true, hormonal changes would only account for a small part of the emotional roller coaster of early motherhood.

The findings don't surprise me.

Despite the wildly different circumstances of my two preg-nancies and two experiences of early motherhood, one thing held true: lack of support and unrealistic cultural expectations conspired to make child-rearing almost impossible. But only *almost*.

In *Letters to a Young Feminist*, the psychologist Phyllis Chesler says it's no coincidence—that in fact mothers are punished by our culture precisely because of the deep power of the experi-ence. When she became a mom, she writes, "I learned that, despite an awful lot of commercial sentimentality, motherhood itself is so powerful, so magical, that it is feared, punished, iso-lated, ghettoized. The experience of pregnancy and motherhood puts you in touch with a more organic, psychic way of being in the world—a way that is more despised than rewarded by our culture. I also learned that mothers did not (were not allowed to) think they were doing anything *that* special, or extraordinary."

Most moms will spend time both in and out of the paid labor force while raising kids. Still, there are plenty of folks who'll try to make us feel guilty about whatever it is we're doing. Stay-at-home and unemployed moms are constantly asked when they plan to return to work. Working moms are constantly hassled about their child-care strategies. But the idea that there's some intrinsic conflict between work and family is beginning to change.

"The work/family-conflict literature focuses on how work conflicts with family and family conflicts with work," says the psychologist Rosalind Chait Barnett, director of the Community, Families, and Work Program at Brandeis University. "Now people are starting to talk about work/family enhancement."

Basically, researchers are finally admitting that work plus family doesn't necessarily equal supermom stress meltdown.

"The dominant theory used to be that multiple roles were bad for women because women had only a limited amount of energy and engaging in multiple roles meant a net loss," Barnett says. "An alternative theory—the expansionist theory—says that having multiple roles actually produces a net gain. Even though you expend energy, you get back psychological, monetary, and other rewards."

To figure out which theory seemed to fit reality, Barnett launched the first large-scale study of two-earner couples and found that two-income families are actually happier, healthier, and better off than two-adult families in which only one partner works for pay.

In a 2001 article in *The American Psychologist*, Barnett and a colleague reviewed two decades' worth of data to confirm that multiple roles bring psychological, physical, and relationship benefits. Several studies they cite counter the idealized view of the happy homemaker. One study found that employed women who moved to part-time work or became homemakers became more depressed. Homemakers who joined the workforce became less depressed. Another study found that while the presence of preschool-aged children in the home was associated with distress for all women, working moms were less distressed than stay-at-homes.

There's a limit to the number of roles we can balance or juggle without getting overloaded. Still, media images haven't quite caught up with the research. "One image you see is the working mom with a cell phone in her ear, briefcase in her hand, and no time for her kids," says Toni S. Zimmerman, a human development and family studies professor and director of the Marriage and Family Therapy program at Colorado State University. "The other mom you see is the one who's home 24/7 baking cookies. You don't see a lot of moms in between, even though that's where most moms are."

Like so many of the moms I interviewed for this book, my most transcendent life memories focus on my relationships with my kids. But the fears and dramas and social isolation of motherhood have also been the source of my greatest anguish. To make matters more complex, very few of us feel empowered to talk honestly about our experiences without couching our complaints in good-natured jokes and "it was all worthwhile."

When I had my daughter, so many people told me I wouldn't be able to handle motherhood that I felt as if I had to hide all my stress and despair. When I had my son, I expected to feel more free, but I noticed right away that friends and acquaintances were just as quick to silence my darker thoughts. "This birth was planned, obviously," they said. "You're so lucky. Your life is perfect." As if being honest about the complexity of it all meant that I wished my son away. As Marcy Sheiner wrote in issue 13 of *Hip Mama*, "I dearly love my children and do not wish them gone. As a matter of fact, it is precisely the love I feel for these people, a complex, many-faceted love unparalleled by any other I have known, that makes the condition of motherhood so unbearable."

When no one was around to make me feel guilty for not enjoying every minute of my new motherhood, I did the job myself. *What did I have to gripe about, anyway?* But we don't do ourselves any favors when we cling to simplistic notions about "happily ever after" and "loving every minute of it."

Plenty of women with children believe that we're happier because of them—and maybe we are and maybe we're not—but it's nonsense to say that we all *need* children in order to evolve into whole and soulful women. What mothers are talking about when we make wild claims like "I'd be incomplete without my kid" is our experience of rising to the occasion in a deep and complex relationship.

If we are to be honest, then, we have to admit that motherhood has made us both happier and more miserable. Motherhood is spiritual highs and deep love, and the institution of motherhood is a locked cage.

"Under patriarchy," Chesler writes, "mothers have no rights, only obligations."

Still, we choose to have children. We do it because mothering is good for the soul. We do it because rising to the occasion in deep and complex relationships is good for the soul. As the writer Mary Karr has pointed out, a dysfunctional family is any family with more than one person in it. And yet, with lovers, partners, spouses, siblings, children, parents, and friends, that's what we do—we build families. We seek relationship. We gauge our moral development by our responsibility to those relation-ships. We are women, and whether nature or nurture has made us this way, these things are true.

In our journals, even when we wrote without planning to share our entries with anyone else, the mothers on my council of experts noted transcendent moments with their kids.

"The baby starting crawling for real," Sonja wrote. "He's a very happy baby."

"Last year at this time I traveled to Greece with Brennan and today I'm more there than here, happy in a memory," Margaret wrote. "In Greece, I was sick with a chest cold but it didn't diminish the magic. She took everything in stride—so different from school days and life at home. We sat for hours in cafés. She colored, named her favorite antiquities better than any adult companion, ate chocolate ice cream, and made friends with a cat."

"I was particularly happy to find out that I was having a daughter," Britt wrote. "The minutes after Piper's birth were amazing. I hadn't realized how overwhelmingly full and com-plete I would feel."

"I was happy when I was sitting with Maia and baby Max on the damp grass outside Maia's apartment building in L.A.," I wrote. "Maia sat in the sun and Max lay on his sea-green blanket in the shade. I spend so much of my time worrying about Maia living so far away. I spend the rest of my time predicting Max's needs. This rare moment when we're all together and I know we're all safe feels like something miraculous."

"The sun came out today," Margaret wrote. "Drank morning coffee on the porch and remembered what it feels like to be warmed by the sun. My daughter played hopscotch and the cats chased circles around her, then stalked each other in the grass."

Consuelo looked forward to visiting her grown child. "I woke up to the songs of birds chirping," she wrote. "I went for a walk in the sunshine—trees blooming, flowers sweet smelling. I got an airline ticket to see Mateo for Mother's Day."

All these moments with children—moments lived outside the confines of the institution of motherhood—gave us pause.

In *Recollections of My Life as a Woman*, the poet Diane di Prima tells of a night at Allen Ginsberg's place in New York. She'd gotten a friend to babysit her young daughter and headed over to Ginsberg's apartment because Jack Kerouac and Philip Whalen were in town for "one of those nights with lots of important intense talk about writing you don't remember later."

Well, Diane had promised her babysitter that she'd be back at 11:30 that night, and 11:30 starts rolling around, so Diane bids her farewells. "Whereupon, Kerouac raised himself up on one elbow on the linoleum and announced in a stentorian voice: 'DI PRIMA, UNLESS YOU FORGET ABOUT YOUR BABYSITTER, YOU'RE NEVER GOING TO BE A WRITER.'"

How do you like that?

Kerouac just props himself up with one arm and drunkenly slaps us with the great fear we all share. He embodies the archetype of the selfish, self-destructive male artist, and he announces that unless we, too, are willing to be irresponsible to our relationships, we'll never quite measure up.

"I considered this carefully, then and later," di Prima writes, "and allowed that at least part of me thought he was right. But nevertheless I got up and went home."

Three cheers for di Prima!

"I'd given my word to my friend," she explains, "and I would keep it. Maybe I was never going to be a writer, but I had to risk it. That was the risk that was hidden (like a Chinese puzzle) inside the other risk of: can I be a single mom and be a poet?"

A serious question, that one. Serious not only for moms but for all of us. Can we be present in our relationships and still do the work we feel called to do? It's like my friend Lynn says: "A woman has to make a real effort not to dissolve into everything that needs her." Our relationships need us, but we don't want to dissolve. We refuse to dissolve, but we choose also to be responsible to our relationships. We're tired of the drunk guy on the linoleum telling us we can't do both. Women have always done both.

Looking back, di Prima recognizes what is true: Had she opted to stay that night, "there would be no poems. That is, the person who would have left a friend hanging who had done her a favor, also wouldn't have stuck through thick and thin to the business of making poems. It is the same discipline throughout."

The same discipline.

And discipline, like motherhood, is good for the soul. Poetry is good for the soul. Responsibility to all our dysfunctional relationships is good for the soul. The archetype of the selfish male artist tells us that we can't manage all these things at once, that we can't be simultaneously responsible to children, babysitters, self, and art, that we have to sacrifice, to abandon—but we know that's a lie.

As I write this, Kerouac has been in his grave for nearly forty years. Diane di Prima is down in San Francisco, mother of five children, author of thirty-five books of poetry and several memoirs, powerhouse, and twenty-first-century radical.

We don't need children to be happy, but motherhood has taught me this: to experience joy, we have to be able to honestly experience darkness, too. In responsibility to relationship, we build bodies of memory and life experience that we can be proud of. Motherhood has taught me that the opposite of happiness isn't struggle. It isn't even depression. The opposite of happiness is fear and obedience.

In *Revolutionary Letters*, di Prima writes, "Be strong. We have the right to make the universe we dream. No need to fear 'science' groveling apology for things as they are, ALL POWER TO JOY, which will remake the world."

Three cheers for di Prima, for motherhood, for the courage to make the universe we dream.

What she meant by happiness, she said, was the following: she meant having (or having had) (or continuing to have) everything. By everything, she meant, first, the children, then a dear person to live with, preferably a man, but not necessarily (by live with, she meant for a long time but not necessarily). Along with and not in preferential order, she required three or four best women friends to whom she could tell every personal fact and then discuss on the widest deepest and most hopeless level, the economy, the constant, unbeatable, cruel war economy, the slavery of the American worker to the idea of that economy, the complicity of male people in the whole structure, the dumbness of men (including her preferred man) on this subject. By dumbness, she meant everything dumbness has always meant: silence and stupidity. By silence she meant refusal to speak; by stupidity she meant refusal to hear. For happiness she required women to walk with. To walk in the city arm in arm with a woman friend (as her mother had with aunts and cousins so many years ago) was just plain essential. Oh! those long walks and intimate talks, better than standing alone on the most admirable mountain or in the handsomest forest or hay-blown field (all of which were certainly splendid occupations for the wind-starved soul).

    —GRACE PALEY, "Midrash on Happiness"

choose your own diagnosis

※

I got in the car this morning and turned on the radio. "Do you feel sad for no apparent reason?" a voice asked. "Do you feel down and depressed most of the day?" When they're not trying to sell us clean-ing products, they're trying to sell us misery. And then a tortured love song came on.

—FROM ARIEL'S JOURNAL

When my best friend was getting her master's degree in psy-chology, we used to sit in her living room, drinking wine and memorizing the *DSM*—the American Psychiatric Association's *Diagnostic and Statistical Manual of Mental Disorders.* We'd laugh as we diagnosed ourselves with mental impairments trivial and grand. On any given day, we had enough symptoms to qualify for a few disorders. We had "caffeine-induced organic mental disorder," "trichotillomania," or maybe an "adjustment disorder with mixed disturbance of emotion." After a few glasses of wine, we could usually convince ourselves that we fit the criteria for some major personality disorder, too. Passive-aggressive or bipolar?

There were serious psychological concerns delineated in the pages of the *DSM*, but there were also plenty of symptoms that seemed more like common human eccentricities than signs of disease. As we became better versed in the language and the concepts listed in the manual, virtually everything we experienced in our lives and everything we observed in others could be seen through that diagnostic lens.

The teachers who wanted us to read the books they'd written were narcissists, the neighbors who looked out their windows were paranoid, our distractible children had attention deficit, and surely the ex-lovers who played rugby with our hearts were suffering from antisocial personality disorders.

We laughed as we read through all the disorders, but as we began to consider deeply which things got listed as insanity and which things didn't, it all started to feel kind of creepy.

There are, for example, plenty of symptoms listed to describe the way you might feel if your village was bombed, but there's no real diagnosis to describe the person who ordered the bombing. Likewise, if you diet to extremes or binge and purge, you might be anorexic or bulimic—but what's the diagnosis for the advertising designer who insists on enforcing a fashion-industry standard that suggests it's beautiful to live on the brink of starvation? As the psychology professor James E. Maddux writes in the *Handbook of Positive Psychology*, "The illness ideology's conception of 'mental disorder' and the various specific DSM categories of mental disorders are not reflections and mappings of psychological facts about people. Instead, they are social artifacts that serve the same sociocultural goals as our constructions of race, gender, social class, and sexual orientation—that of maintaining and expanding the power of certain individuals and institutions and maintaining social order, as defined by those in power."

The tools of modern psychology are vast, but everything vast has a shadow.

Each time we learn something new about human nature or invent a new way of thinking about it, we have to ask: *Will this information be used for liberation or exploitation? Will it be used to heal us or to make us feel crazy and alone? Will it be used to empower us or to keep us in our places?*

Why aren't psychology students given textbooks full of all the ways in which people can be healthy, soulful, and ever evolving?

Linda, a psychology student in her mid-thirties on my council of experts, wrote in her journal: "There seem to be different kinds of happiness—surprise, delight, new experiences, accomplishment, resourcefulness, aesthetics, art, culture, meaning, love, positive feedback, connection, tactile, holding my children, mother-pride, things getting better, hope, finding my niche, growth, humor, comfort, sensual pleasures, nature, doing what's right, life-giving, the excitement of possibilities, kinship, fun, and pride at having made it this far."

Why isn't there a giant required textbook that expands on each of these various kinds of happiness? Instead of narcissistic and antisocial, we could diagnose ourselves and each other as "tactile and fun" or "predominantly inspired by art and humor."

How is it that psychology—once envisioned as a great healing art—has gotten to this place where our neuroses are considered so much more valid than our resiliences?

Even when psychology isn't used against us, many of the women I talked with hoped for something more forward-focused than traditional therapy.

"My forays into therapy have been exercises in frustration," Margaret said. "They were helpful in the sense that I found out how limited that realm was for me. I want an action plan. What are known ways that people have pulled themselves up and out of difficulties like mine? How have they built the self-esteem that they didn't have? That's what I want to know."

"What seems to be lacking is an active, dynamic, and alive psychological school of thought that can evolve to fit a person's growth and ever-changing needs," Linda said. "When it comes to a psychology of the future or a liberation psychology, I think something more holistic and tailored to the individual is necessary. It seems like life coaching is flirting with the concept. Counseling needs to be synthesized with nutrition, exercise, environmental overhaul, and other wisdom traditions. It could be a living, breathing process that unfolds."

Calliope, whom I invited to join the council of experts because people described her as "chronically blissed," explained how she built her own holistic action plan. "I've been doing these six-month evaluations ever since I was in high school," she said. "I gave myself a journal just for these six-month evaluations—I do my evaluations in December and June. I have specific topics, and I write under each topic. Then I put it away. When I open the journal again six months later, I write first, and then I read back through the old entries. It helps me to discover patterns and see where I am, where I was, and where I want to be. Topics lately have been work, money, learning, family, relatives, love, health, spirituality, living situation, and an overview of my intentions. This is how my 'ten-week plan' came about. Two years ago I was spiraling big-time into darkness, and I didn't know what to do, so I called in the professionals. I was determined to not have the same issues in my December entry. I went to acupuncture and had a massage once a week. I went to holographic repatterning for six sessions. I met with an art therapist twice and started an art installation project that reflects my ever-changing self. I went to my cognitive behavioral therapist through the whole process. I paid for everything in advance, so I knew I would show up. And by prepaying, I got some sweet deals. I moved beyond things. It was extremely intense to *go there*, but worth it."

After our liberation psychology forum, I had to look up Calliope's "holographic repatterning." I imagined colored lights and fancy holographic images, but it's just one of the various energetic and linguistic techniques—like affirmation, autosuggestion, and hypnosis—that are often used in life coaching and other eclectic practices in an attempt to change negative belief patterns that seem to limit us.

All right, I decide. It's time to bite the bullet, embrace my inner dork, and call a life coach of my own. I dial up the longtime coach LaSara Firefox to make an appointment. She can talk with me on Thursday at 2:00 p.m., she says.

I mark my calendar.

Life coaching has its roots in business executive coaching rather than in psychotherapy, but there's an incredible variety when it comes to what different coaches offer, what they charge, and how they practice. There's no central governing body for the profession, but several self-appointed accreditation associations are recognized in the field. The difference between coaching and traditional therapy, Firefox tells me in an e-mail, is that "traditional talk therapy is about looking at your past and figuring out how you got here; life coaching is about looking forward to where you want to be." She warns that a lot of life coaches aren't qualified to deal with childhood trauma, but some practitioners combine psychotherapy with coaching.

Firefox typically starts coaching clients with a three-month commitment, she explains. The commitment consists of hour-long telephone sessions every two weeks, assignments for "action steps" in between those sessions, and e-mail check-ins along the way. "A lot of women come to me to talk about balancing business and family responsibilities," she says, "but I often find that by the time a woman is ready to ask for help, she's already so frazzled—so the first commitment will be around taking care of the self. I find there's a lot of self-judgment and guilt about *ever* choosing business or career over relationship, so first we focus on rebuilding the primary relationship with the self."

When I call back for my consultation on Thursday afternoon, I expect to begin by presenting Firefox with some of the facts of my current life, but she starts right in by asking me about the future. "Where do you see yourself in three months?"

I've just been accepted into a graduate school program to work on a second master's degree, I tell her, but I'm not sure the program's quite right for me. Ideally, within three months, I'll know if I want to move forward with the school thing, and if I choose school, I'll be getting started. "And," I add, almost as an aside, "I'm ready to make more money."

"And five years from now?"

To my initial surprise, this question is easier for me. A clear vision springs to mind: My daughter has graduated from college, and she's excited about her new life. My son has started school himself. I'm free from all this credit card debt and working on publishing projects and all things that inspire me instead of spending all my energy worrying about the kids' tuition payments and the mortgage.

The vision is clear, but the path isn't. *How do I get there?*

Firefox and I talk for an hour, and she gives me some concrete "action steps." She wants me to research a few of the ideas I've floated in our telephone consultation, and she wants me to do a writing exercise.

"Writing? I can do that."

"Write your ideal scene for your life five years from now,"
she instructs. "Write it in the present tense as if you're already
there. And then, once you've got a couple of pages, go ahead
and look back and describe how you got there."

It seems simple, but I'm inexplicably energized after our telephone session.

I've always been attracted to goal-free living—the idea of
catching a wave and just riding it—but this simple scene, projected five years into the future, catches my imagination. My
ideal scene could be *anything*.

What if anything is possible?

Anything.

After a year and a half of keeping my happiness journal, this
futurizing exercise feels like a natural next step. It's as if I've been
collecting seeds all these months and now I'm ready to plant
a few.

As I'm working, as I'm driving to the grocery store, as I'm
lathering shampoo into the baby's wispy hair, I envision futures.
I become preoccupied with possibilities in the same way talk
therapy once hooked me and fascinated me with all the scenarios of my past. In five years, I could have a printing press. I could
be writing epic plays. In five years, I might feel comfortable in
my skin. Pay off my student loans. Relax a little. In five years, I
might have grandchildren.

I don't know if coaching is right for me—I'm skeptical of a
profession that's totally unregulated—but I'm also intrigued. The
years-long training of psychologists holds a certain comfort, but
I don't want to consider my past anymore. This comes as a relief
and a revelation. I rinse the shampoo from the baby's head, and
he looks a little surprised. *I do not want to consider the past anymore!*

I already know about my past. I've talked about it, written

about it, processed it. I understand the ways in which pain and abuse have built me. I know where I've screwed up. I honor the parts of myself that have been taken for granted, lied to, belittled. I'm proud of all that I've accomplished.

But the past is the past.

And here I am tonight. The baby's gone to sleep, and I've got clean pajamas on. It's still light outside, late as it is. And I'm looking forward to longer days still.

Surely I've got problems enough to fill any diagnostic manual. I'm anxious, I'm repressed, I'm neurotic, I'm acting out—aren't you? I'm addicted, I'm paranoid, I'm narcissistic, I'm passive-aggressive.

But maybe it's more important that I'm expansive. I'm courageous. I'm ambitious. I'm inspired. I'm generous. I'm prolific. And I'm writing this book as a living and breathing love letter to *you.*

Because you know what I mean.

You get it.

I know you do.

THE SIXTH QUESTION
When was the last time you felt inspired?

When I asked women to recall the last time they felt inspired or energized, their answers captured an amazing range of experience. They thought of creative acts, moments of beauty in the natural world, their own accomplishments, and the accomplishments of others. They thought of activism, Sunday school, unexpected expressions of love, and quick reprieves from anger.

I've decided to become an artist again after several years. I've started playing music with a friend, and I've started painting a little. Making art and being creative give me a jolt. It amazes me how I really let the years go by without making anything.

Yesterday, my husband and I went on a long walk with our two little dogs. We walked on the beach. We climbed over mossy rocks and sea cliffs when the sand was unpassable, and we had a most lovely time. We talked and laughed and recharged our batteries from a long week of hosting guests.

I received a package of supplies in the mail yesterday and immediately took it into my darkroom to try out the new technique—tintypes, which I find really exciting and inspiring. It's a wonderful feeling to have the chance to explore a photographic method that is so traditional and ties me to the past.

I got an unexpected compliment from my partner. I was washing dishes, and he said, "Oh, look, your hair is so pretty!" He sounded like a different person from the one I've been living with for sixteen years.

We are building a house right now and, in part to save money and in part because I can't find things that I like, I have recently made a few light fixtures to go inside. They're nothing fancy, but this creative process really energizes me, and it inspires me to do more, imperfect projects.

I saw a documentary about the architect Frank Gehry. That inspired me. To think of the amazing things you can build from some small seed in your imagination.

I made some beautiful posters.

I went to see three short experimental films at UC Santa Cruz with my sweetie, and we had inspired conversation about film and art and stuff on the way home, including ideas that we've had for films we would make someday.

I went with a friend to try out a new restaurant. It was packed. The crowd was young. The food was lovely, and the buzz of people around was exciting. We came out energized, and now I want to explore more new places.

This morning I went shopping for a door for our house. I found locally produced doors in my neighborhood with locally grown wood in a style that suits. Normally, consumer purchases don't excite me, but when they align with my eco-values, they do.

I went to an orientation of volunteers, which is related to my work. Their collective energy was inspiring, and I fed off their idealism like a parasite. I loved hearing about the ways they were going to help people get themselves out of poverty.

Seeing Beth Ditto on the cover of Bust Magazine*! Her career is so inspiring. That was my number-one most excited, inspired moment. Seeing her succeed and stay a loudmouthed, fat-positive, queer feminist.*

A drive to the grocery store with my son along the Rio Grande in full fall color. I'm a simple person when it comes to getting energized.

I learned to ferment—very empowering. We made tempeh, we pressed six bushels of apples into hard cider, we made a huge crock of sauerkraut, and then we made banana wine.

My sister and I just started teaching Sunday school. There is a purity about the way children think of the divine. Hearing their voices lift up in song is the definition of "joyful noise."

money magnetism

✺

I was happy to get paid, happy to be busy at work.
—FROM SONJA'S JOURNAL

I can't rationally afford it, but I sign up for three months of life coaching on faith.

In our first session after the initial consultation, Firefox leads me through what she calls a "values elicitation"—she asks me a series of stealthy questions designed to draw out the priorities I've built my life around. We come up with a collage of things I hold important: my kids, creative work, relaxation, relationships, righteousness, service, and spirituality.

"I think it's important to note something that's glaringly missing from your field of values," Firefox tells me.

I think hard, but I can't come up with anything that's missing.

"What's missing?"

"Money."

Far-out, I think. *Could it be that I don't value money?*

With the baby at home and my daughter in college, I've certainly been feeling the squeeze. Just to stay afloat—to avoid slipping ever deeper into debt—I needed to double my income. But every time I've made a move to increase my cash flow, all my nagging little beliefs about money started bobbing to the surface: *Money is the root of all evil. If I charge too much for my work, the people I really want to serve won't be able to afford me. My work isn't worth much, anyway. I get to do the work I love—writing and teaching and editing—what right do I have to demand to be paid? Hard labor is work. This isn't work. Anyway, money is dirty. Good, spiritual people have no need for money. Why should I need it?*

"If you say those bad things about money," my friend Inga Muscio once scolded me, "money will get its feelings hurt, and money will NOT want to come around!"

I knew she was right, but what's a girl to do about her deeply held beliefs? I was raised by a hippie-era starving artist from Beverly Hills and a Catholic priest who'd taken a vow of poverty after the childhood trauma of the Great Depression, so I guess I wasn't exactly taught to put money concerns first. And I guess my big rebellion against a world I've seen as overly materialistic has been to charge as little as possible for my work.

"Listen," Firefox says the next time we talk. "I come from the same countercultural belief sets you're echoing, but I honestly believe that this is the next area of emancipation for the women's movement. Until we can get out of debt, pay for health care, build a retirement fund, and keep a roof over our heads the whole time, we will not be truly independent."

Money as emancipation. I'd never thought of it that way. We don't need to imagine that money alone will buy us happiness, but maybe refusing to take money seriously isn't the empowered alternative. Money anxiety, it turns out, can hit women hard. According to a 2008 report from the American Psychological Association, "The declining state of the nation's economy is taking a physical and emotional toll on people nationwide, and it is women who are bearing the brunt of financial stress."

During a recession, according to the Joint Economic Committee of the Senate, women are particularly vulnerable to job loss. For those who have jobs, the wage gap between men and women has actually increased in some areas in recent years. If workingwomen earned the same salaries as workingmen with the same education and experience, our family incomes would rise by four thousand dollars a year and poverty rates would be cut in half. Interestingly, the gender wage gap exists even among self-employed women like me. In other words, even when we set our own rates, we tend to ask for less than our male colleagues who do the same work. Talk about internalized oppression.

For the women on my council of experts, spending and earning money came up in our journals quite often. Jennifer noted "a special kind of shopping happiness," and who doesn't know what she's talking about?

Linda summed up the highlight of one day, saying, "I scored huge! Garage sale—they weren't even done bringing out the stuff—six animated movies and two cute kid's chairs for ten bucks. Harlan and Louis loved the new delights."

A little bit of materialism made us happy.

But more often, the subject of money came up in the context of *un*happiness—in the context of fear, of lack, of anxiety. "I'm just tired," Akiko wrote. "Up all night trying to figure out how I'm going to pay the bills."

We worried about overspending, about not being able to manage the money we did have, about taking care of our families. Some of the women who worried about money were poor, but most were middle-income, living above their means or unclear on exactly what their "means" were. Money is a language of power, after all, and one that many of us still feel uncomfortable with. As women, we've been socialized to feel incompetent when it comes to money. And many of us have reacted to an overly money-focused culture by closing our eyes to the value of money entirely.

But maybe there's a healthier approach.

When we feel competent in our financial lives, after all, we feel in control of our destinies. The financial guru Suze Orman insists that the respect we show our money is a direct reflection of the respect we feel for ourselves. Kind of scary, but true. If we can develop a more honest relationship with money, then perhaps we can step into a new level of power and sense of self-worth.

When my friend Inga Muscio went off to college, she noticed right away that the kids from upper-class backgrounds seemed to have a wholly different attitude toward money from the kids who grew up poor. She started paying closer attention. *What might she learn from her new, entitled friends?*

"People who grew up with money have a welcoming attitude about it," Muscio discovered. "They welcome money into their lives. People who grew up poor tend to have a lot of negative associations with money—they associate money with money *problems*."

Muscio made a conscious effort to revamp her relationship with money.

We were hanging around with a lot of starving artists at the time, and she made it her mission to teach any who would listen her theory of money magnetism. "Repeat after Inga," she said. "I am a money magnet. Money flows naturally and *easily* into my life." And then she threw her arms into the air and smiled kind of maniacally as she bellowed on: "Money stays awake at night thinking about me! Money is sexually attracted to me!"

Soon the community was abuzz with this simple new idea about cash flow. "I used Inga's attitude that money is really super-duper and good," says the artist Eli Halpin. "I always felt like I was supposed to hate money, but once I let go of that ridiculous feeling, I acquired a healthy relationship with it and the freedoms it brings, and I began to let it flood into my life. I adore money now. Money has enabled me to rescue animals and people and to take care of myself. I can supplement my sister's college mission, and I can afford to visit my family."

"To me poor people are like bonsai trees," the economics professor Muhammad Yunus said in his 2006 Nobel lecture. "When you plant the best seed of the tallest tree in a flowerpot, you get a replica of the tallest tree, only inches tall. There is nothing wrong with the seed you planted, it is only the soil-base that is too inadequate. Poor people are bonsai people. There is nothing wrong with their seeds. Simply, society never gave them a base to grow on."

Back in the 1980s, Yunus had founded the Grameen Bank in Bangladesh and pioneered "microcredit," an innovative program that provides poor people with small loans to launch independent businesses. Microcredit has since spread to every continent, and today there's a Grameen-type bank in almost every country.

In defiance of the old-school Bangladeshi banking system, which treated women as second-class borrowers, the Grameen Bank set out to loan money to women and men on an equal basis, but bank founders soon discovered that women were more effective agents of change. When extra income came into a household through the woman, the children's diet, the family's health, and the household repairs got first priority. Men were more likely to spend some of their money down at the tavern. Women also turned out to be more creditworthy—we repaid our loans. But the most compelling reason to treat women as priority clients was in the Grameen Bank's mandate itself: to lend to the poorest first. And women represented the poorest of the poor. Ninety-seven percent of the bank's borrowers are now women, repayment rates are near 100 percent, and bank borrowers become bank owners when they repay their loans and begin saving.

"I don't understand why anybody should be poor on this planet," Yunus said in a 2003 interview. "There is more than enough to make everybody happy—not by giving things away, but by enhancing the capability of each person and by creating an enabling environment. There is enough inside each person to take care of himself or herself."

Yunus believes that the dynamics of capitalism can be applied to solve virtually all the world's problems. In *Creating a World Without Poverty*, he maps out his idea for consciously created social business—a model that uses the vibrancy of the free market to tackle everything from poverty to pollution. "We get what we want, or what we don't refuse," he said in his Nobel lecture. "If we firmly believe that poverty is unacceptable to us, and that it should not belong to a civilized society, we would have built appropriate institutions and policies to create a poverty-free world. We wanted to go to the moon, so we went there. We achieve what we want to achieve. If we are not achieving something, it is because we have not put our minds to it. We create what we want."

We create what we value.

In the March 2008 issue of *Bust Magazine*, Tara Bracco sheds light on the concept of a "Fuck You Fund." I'd never heard the phrase before, but right away I liked it. A "stash of cash that allows you to ditch a crappy job or a harmful relationship without money being an obstacle. It's cooler and more empowering than an emergency fund, because it enables you to make proactive, healthy choices about your life."

I'd heard of mad money—the twenty dollars my grandmother always warned me to have in my wallet so I could get a taxi home "if the fellow who takes you out gets fresh." I was also familiar with the hidden cash that advocates for victims of domestic violence recommend that we keep even if we're not immediately ready to leave abusive partners. Two hundred dollars sewn into the seam of a coat might mean the difference between having to stay in a violent home on a winter night and being able to catch a bus and get a hotel room. But a whole fund? In a bank account? For employed and independent women not living in dire circumstances?

Yes.

"The FU Fund is the financial equivalent of a mental health day," says Manisha Thakor, a co-author of *On My Own Two Feet: A Modern Girl's Guide to Personal Finance.* "It's about taking back the power and saying, 'I deserve to be happy.'"

The idea of an FU Fund is nothing new—but it's mostly been talked about by men in business school. Financially independent guys might not think about mad money to escape bad dates or domestic violence worst-case scenarios, but they know that they'll need money if they want to quit their jobs. Why isn't the term part of the female vernacular? Women are more likely to think in terms of an emergency fund, Thakor says. As a result, we're hesitant to use our savings in ways that might further our goals or our own happiness because it feels irresponsible to spend "emergency" money when there's no life-threatening emergency.

But what would happen if we took ourselves out of survival mode? What's wrong with giving ourselves the freedom to make proactive choices *and* to respond to unexpected emergencies?

The right amount of savings varies for each of us, but Thakor says it makes good sense to shoot for three months' worth of essential living expenses reserved in an emergency fund and three months' worth of expenses set aside in a Fuck You Fund. With this level of financial security, we'll never feel stuck in bad professional or personal situations. We'll always have access to the implements of our escape.

Establishing new funds for freedom requires that we've got some expendable income, of course, but, more important, it requires us to begin to see money as a tool of empowerment rather than as something we needn't worry our pretty little heads about.

I make a plan, cut up my credit cards, raise my rates for free-lance work.

I write my daughter's college tuition check, get health insurance for both kids.

Emancipation is not the same as greed.

Pretty soon I get a windfall. I put half of it into my new Fuck You Fund, and then I buy a giant painting by a local artist, hang it on my bedroom wall, and open my eyes every morning to a little family of hobo birds making stew at a campfire. Money is emancipation. And money is being able to support the artists in my community with a picture of warmth and security.

one day while i was doing the laundry

※

*I realize that as I'm recording these moments of happiness, I actually
attract more happiness into my life. This process of noticing has
become a process of invoking. It's so simple, but I've never asked
myself like this, on a daily basis, What do I want? I guess I just
expected to wake up happy one day. Now I'm creating a road map.*
— FROM AKIKO'S JOURNAL

I've spent many months trying out everything I learned about at
last fall's Positive Psychology Summit. I've meditated at the Buddhist priory in my neighborhood. I've gone to independent
movies and community art shows for inspiration. I've thrown
myself into my work. I've listed my accomplishments, recalled
the feelings I expected them to bring and the feelings they did
bring. I've spent time with my baby, escaped to the coast for a
long weekend with friends. I've traveled to Miami and measured
the effect the weather and the traffic have on my mood. I've
pored over the subjective interview answers women gave me
when I asked them about happiness. I've categorized and quan-
tified their reported fulfillment, utilized my skills of statistical
analysis. I've paged through my own happiness journal and tal-
lied how often I found happiness in nature, how often in work,
how often in relationship. I've measured the ways in which my

level of contentment correlated with my income. It isn't on my list, but as springtime blooms into summer, I decide that it's only fair to give the old-school prescription for female happiness a try. As Dr. S. Weir Mitchell advised Charlotte Perkins Gilman back in the 1880s, I resolve to become as domestic as possible.

I perfect my recipe for peach-berry pie, then consider the house. At first I worry that my domestic motives are impure. This is an opportunity to get the place cleaned up while still, technically, working on my book. It's a line of thinking that smacks of the "career girl" my grandmother warned me against becoming. But what can I do? Despite my grandmother's valiant efforts, my aversion to domesticity runs deep. I blame Carol Channing. She poisoned me against becoming some lady who smiles while she scours and scrubs and mops and cleans when I was just a wee and impressionable young thing. She preached to me from my favorite 1970s album, *Free to Be . . . You and Me*, and in that husky squeal of hers assured me that my mommy hated housework, my daddy hated housework, and when I grew up, so would I.

But maybe Carol had it wrong.

I pick up *The American Woman's Home* and read the words of Catharine Beecher and Harriet Beecher Stowe, great abolitionist intellectuals who also wrote this 1869 Victorian tome on how to be a good woman and wife. And they promise me that housekeeping is my ticket to bliss. All I need is "a right appreciation of this mission, and a proper performance of these duties." If I do everything right, "true happiness will be the reward."

True happiness.

I decide to begin in my basement laundry room, where giant piles of clothes and towels and bedding, loosely separated into lights and darks, clean and unclean, tower unmoving like a museum installation.

The baby is sleeping in his crib, so I creep downstairs, slip a Loretta Lynn CD into the player, and begin to fold, sort, and pile. It makes me happy to handle the baby's little white T-shirts and soft blue jeans. His smallness is so dear. I find a few of my daughter's things in the clean pile, too. I'm happy that she'll be home from school for a long weekend soon. I put a load of darks in the machine to wash, keep folding.

About an hour into my project, Maria gets home from work and finds me in the long-neglected laundry room. "What are you doing down here?" she wants to know.

"I'm testing the theory of domesticity."

She raises an eyebrow. "How does it work?"

"I just have to be as domestic as possible and then jot down my thoughts whenever I notice I'm happy."

She nods. She is by now accustomed to my strange behavior, my testing of hypotheses toward a general theory of happiness. "And how's it going?"

"Surprisingly well," I have to admit. But I can also recall afternoons spent down here in the dark of the basement when I felt more oppressed than wistful.

In *A Life of One's Own*, Marion Milner describes what she calls an "internal gesture" that seemed to transform her experiences from mundane to meditative. When we're trying to flip that switch, our motives do matter. "I'm happy here folding the laundry," I explain, "but it's because I don't *have to* be here. I just feel like it. I've got a higher purpose. I'm looking for the secret to happiness. And I'm in no hurry. I'm loafing with this laundry."

The baby squeaks from his crib and knocks on the wall the

way he does when he's ready to join the awake. Maria heads upstairs to fetch him.

Mihaly Csikszentmihalyi's flow theory holds that having a higher purpose is key to achieving optimal experience, and I realize that maybe this was Beecher and Beecher Stowe's point in *The American Woman's Home*. These days they'd probably have to call their book *The Dharma and Zen of Housework* to sell any copies, but the basic idea is the same: If we see our work as indentured servitude, we're sunk. If we choose to see it as a calling and imbue it with positive spiritual and psychological meaning, we're apt to find joy in it. There's no reward for being nice in oppressive circumstances, of course, but laundry isn't *intrinsically* oppressive. And there's something deliciously Zen in that rare moment when the laundry is all folded, you know?

I start to space out. I'm folding, but mostly I'm thinking about all these things, thinking about all the things I've written about in my happiness journal over the months, thinking about whether my friends will judge my project as silly, and then, all of a sudden, out of the clear blue of my mind's eye, all the inked and penciled entries of my happiness journal seem to rearrange themselves into a rounded pattern. The thousands of pages of happiness studies I've read—conflicting as they sometimes seemed—all synchronize themselves into that basic arrangement, too. All the voices of the women I've interviewed come together into a strangely harmonized chorus: In nature, with our friends or children, working or reading, we are happy when we are dynamically engaged with our lives. We are happy when we're following threads of thought and activity we're curious about—unconcerned where those threads will lead. In her 1938 book *If You Want to Write*, Brenda Ueland put it this way: "I discovered that you should feel when writing, not like Lord Byron on a mountaintop, but like a child stringing beads in kinder-garten—happy, absorbed, and quietly putting one bead on after another." Whatever we're doing, we are happy when we feel like children stringing beads. We are happy when we're not trying to change ourselves.

"I was happy when I was driving across the bridge and the sun was shining," I wrote in my journal early in the project. "I was on my way to pick up a quilt for the baby and to find an obscure academic psychology text—the domestic and the cone-headed." I am consistently happy when I experience a particular synthesis of the intellectual and the domestic. I like geeky aca-demic texts and I like berry pie. I am happy when something garden-variety and everyday inspires grand artistic ideas. My friend Lynn's paintings of tomatoes make me happy.

Theories of hedonic adaptation tend to emphasize the nega-tive side of our human tendency to adjust to new circumstances, extrapolating from that truth that we're all a bunch of ne'er-do-wells who'll never be satisfied—always reaching for some reced-ing horizon, pursuing but never attaining. In that context, the quest for happiness seems futile. But what if happiness is a mov-ing force—a force we can move with?

We all know that there's no such thing as "happily ever after," but how many of us still live with our hearts set on that static fantasy? It's like what Simone de Beauvoir said in the introduc-tion to *The Second Sex*: "Those who are condemned to stagna-tion are often pronounced happy on the pretext that happiness consists in being at rest. This notion we reject."

In fact, happiness usually consists in being in motion.

I think of the psychiatrist R. D. Laing's cryptic truth: "The life I am trying to grasp is the me that is trying to grasp it." And now I understand his words in a new way: the happiness we are trying to grasp is the experience of trying to grasp it.

As Antoine de Saint-Exupéry wrote in *The Little Prince*, "It is the time you have wasted for your rose that makes your rose so important."

Among the hundreds of women I interviewed, there was no obvious demographic variable that made the difference between those who considered themselves happy and those who did not. Women with children weren't happier than those without. It didn't seem to matter much where we lived or whether or not we took cream in our coffee. Some women with traditional values and breadwinning husbands were happy; some felt trapped and stifled. Some single feminists with dogs were happy; some felt lonely and duped by the promises of an unfinished revolution. Women who had a spiritual practice did rank themselves happier than the agnostics and the atheists, but faith wasn't a deal breaker. My findings often mirrored established positive psychological data when it came to all these easily measured variables, but there was a deeper, more subtle pattern. What the women who considered themselves happy had in common was more psychic than demographic. The women who reported being the happiest were the women who had the self-esteem, the basic resources, and the courage to question—and often reject—the scripts for female happiness they had been handed. Whether those scripts were Victorian, 1950s TV–traditional, or modern feminist, these women had been able to step back and consider their own desires outside the boundaries of established expectations.

When I asked women to describe decisions they'd made primarily based on their own well-being, the pattern became crystal clear. The women who were happy talked about leaving spouses despite familial and cultural pressure to stay, or they described choosing relationships over career *despite* feminist values. The women who were happy talked about going back to school in the face of a partner's opposition, or they described moving to a new city even when close friends felt abandoned. The women who were happy described standing up for themselves and choosing to keep children they were told to give up for adoption, or they described the opposite—the deeply personal decision not to have or not to keep children they didn't feel equipped to care for. Many of these women had spent some portion of their lives—a season or a decade—in active rebellion against cultural norms. Many still lived in what they saw as continuous and disciplined resistance. But saying no to expectations was just the beginning. The women who were happy weren't the ones who seemed to get stuck in rebellion and postmodern commitment phobia, but rather those who were able to take it further—to write new scripts for themselves. In the spirit of curiosity and experimentation, they had freed themselves from the past and were willing to commit to new paths and new visions. The women who were happy were optimists, but they weren't perfectionists. In some cases, they had failed in profound ways, but they had failed on their own terms. The quality that predicted happiness, then, was a kind of openness—a childlike curiosity coupled with a very grown-up understanding of self-respect and self-protection.

"I grew up battling naysayers," one twentysomething woman told me. She grew up with a supportive single mom, but her faultfinding father, who hovered on the periphery of her life, was quick to make her feel small and unpretty. Her stepsisters and stepbrothers were tall and blond, went to sleepaway camp, dated successfully, played tennis, and seemed well-adjusted. Determined not to stand in their shadows, she became fiercely competitive in the things she was good at: school, close friendships, working. She approached her professional life with plenty of love and joy, but also with some zealotry—and the intense need to prove herself. She spent her college years taking care of her parents, both of whom had fallen ill, and feeling as if she was everybody's caretaker. It was a double-edged sword: she enjoyed caring for others and experienced real fulfillment from it, but she also ended up feeling as if too much of her energy was spent figuring out other people's problems. "Then about a year ago I decided to take a hard look at my personal life," she said. "I had the job I'd always wanted. I'd ended a long-term relationship with a wonderful but troubled man. I'd quit drinking. Everything should have felt right, but something was wrong: I was anxious nearly all the time. I started fretting about money, even though I lived within my modest means and always had. Suddenly I'd become the kind of girl who obsessed over cleaning her apartment and checked her bank balance at six o'clock in the morning in fits of panic. I worked nearly all the time, sometimes into the wee hours on Saturday nights. Something had to give." Instead of letting that something take her by surprise, she jumped right into several of her biggest fears: the fear of self-care and the fear of spending too much money. She took all her savings and booked a yoga retreat in Mexico. She practiced yoga for three hours a day and forgot about her job. She ran on the beach in the mornings and read for pleasure for the first time since she'd graduated from college. "I was alone," she said. "I was tan. And I came home so much happier." More important, she integrated the things that made her happy in Mexico into her daily life. "In the last year, I've deepened my yoga practice, started volunteering again, gotten more involved in the vegan and raw food community, become more open to making new friends, and learned how to put work aside on the weekends. Sure, I'm still neurotic and a workaholic, but I've learned how to be those things and still chill out once in a while. And it's done me wonders."

In the travel memoir *Off the Map*, the authors Hib Chickena and Kika Kat write, "This is what it means to be an adventurer in our day: to give up creature comforts of the mind, to realize possibilities of imagination. Because everything around us says no you cannot do this, you cannot live without that, nothing is useful unless it is in service to money, to gain, to stability. The adventurer gives in to the tides of chaos, trusts the world to support her—and in doing so turns her back on the fear and obedience she has been taught. She rejects the indoctrination of impossibility. My adventure is a struggle for freedom."

Maria saunters back into the laundry room now, baby on her hip. "How's it going?" she wants to know.

I haven't made much further progress with the clothes.

The baby smiles with his whole face. He's all radiance and inspiration these days. I can't remember what it feels like to sleep for more than four hours at a stretch, but something about the light behind the baby's eyes reminds me of my stepfather. I kiss his apple cheek. He turns away, suddenly shy.

I think back to the way I felt at the beginning of this project—not depressed, exactly, but lulled into a kind of good-enough stagnation. I longed for the inspiration I'd felt way back in my freshman year of college, when I still believed in the limitlessness of possibility. Since then, I've discovered that the act of turning our backs on fear and obedience—the act of opening to a dynamic engagement with life—isn't some onetime act we complete in our youth but a constant and delicious adventure. Always grasping, always in motion.

Happiness, like some central seed, is actually contained within the pursuit.

THE SEVENTH QUESTION
Are you happier than you were this time last year?

❋

When I first asked women what they thought would make them happier, they mentioned money, professional recognition, engaging work, and strong relationships. They wished for good health, romance, creative projects, more time, or fewer responsibilities. Every season brings changes, so it seemed only fair that I ask again. Are you happier or less happy than you were this time last year? And what seemed to make the difference?

I'm happier. There have been huge changes in my life, the biggest one being having a baby. The baby just fills me with love. Going through the pregnancy with my partner and now having the baby together also has done wonders for our relationship. We are more present, trusting, and honest with each other.

Oh, a thousand times happier! I got divorced from a selfish narcissist and got away from his violent adult children. I was inspired by this experience to start a show called The Dick Monologues, *which has been having a great deal of success here in Austin. And one of the other cast members brought her ex-boyfriend to the show, and he asked me out afterward, so now, thanks to my ex-husband's idiocy, I'm having roman-*

tic and theatrical success. Oh, and I lost forty pounds on the divorce diet, which, sorry about the cliché about women like to weigh less, but I actually do like weighing less.

I think I am happier. There are several reasons but the biggest is probably that my daughter, now two, is more independent. Having her be able to play on her own and "with" other children not only frees up a little of my time but just makes me happy—I like to see her progressing and growing.

I am happier. Last year at this time, my daughter had moved back in with us and she was a mess. We were caring for her six-year-old son, and, as much as we love him, our lives were stressed to the max with all the turmoil surrounding my daughter's dilemma. This year she is in a stable relationship, has a good job, and is living in her own home and caring for her son. My husband and I are back to our relatively carefree existence.

I am happier this year—it's all about family and friends. My happiness also depends on my husband's, and he has sold eighteen paintings over the last six months and did a few commissions, so that's very good.

I think I'm happier now, more fulfilled in my work, and I've made great progress toward realizing some dreams I always knew I had, and also realizing some hope I didn't know I had. I've been really validated by my family, got named a godmother, and my friends have really demonstrated their love and affection for me very clearly in ways that are easy for me to see and receive.

Slightly less happy. We are trying to get pregnant, and it has been a very loaded and difficult process for me.

Much happier. I am on sabbatical in India, where I find myself crying in gratitude at least once daily. The bliss comes from the gratitude as the two are related. That is, the direct amount of happiness in one's life is correlated to the amount of gratitude one has. I had to let go of many fears to reach this place. I try not to get stuck in how I will make this new place work when I return to life in Portland. Then again, I realize I have very little interest in the life I had. That life didn't leave room for being present.

Less happy. The developer that owns my building wants everyone to relocate and is offering very little assistance for the families to find affordable housing in this neighborhood where our kids go to school.

My good fortune of last year is still with me. I inherited five thousand dollars. Now I still have two hundred dollars in my savings account and five hundred dollars in my checking. That's a buffer I've never had before.

I am happier today than I was a year ago, without question. I am living in community and on a piece of land as opposed to in a city apartment, I'm growing food, I've made great strides as a communicator, I'm physically stronger and healthier, and I'm having way more sex.

imperfectly

※

I'm actually happy to be the person that I'm turning out to be because I feel real.

—FROM JENNIFER'S JOURNAL

On a beautiful spring day in 1982, when he was thirty-eight years old, Philip Brickman, the man who did the famous lottery winners study and came up with the "hedonic treadmill" concept to explain why humans pursue but never seem to attain happiness, climbed to the top of the tallest building in Ann Arbor, Michigan, and jumped.

According to his obituary, one of his favorite topics of discussion was what constituted "the perfect day."

But happiness, as we have learned, doesn't mean that our days are perfect. And happiness, life reminds us, does not mean the absence of sadness. It doesn't mean the absence of suffering.

The Buddhists' first noble truth says it simply: "Life is suffering." Psychologists are now turning to modern Buddhists in their ongoing quest for the secret of joy.

Maybe happiness requires that we understand there is no perfect day.

Maybe it's when we begin to accept things as they are that they begin to change.

When University of Wisconsin scientists mapped the brain of the Buddhist monk Matthieu Ricard as he meditated, the pictures showed excessive activity in the left prefrontal cortex, the area just inside the forehead associated with joy and enthusiasm. People with happy temperaments generally exhibit a high ratio of activity in the left prefrontal cortex. Those who are prone to anxiety, fear, and depression show more activity in the right prefrontal cortex. The degree to which the left side of Ricard's brain lit up far surpassed that in the 150 other subjects researchers had measured. Ricard, who had more than thirty years' experience in contemplative practice, might have exhibited the same results before he became a monk, but given that his readings were truly off the chart, scientists surmised that meditation serves to mold our brains and help us develop happier and less-afflicted temperaments.

The most influential twentieth-century Western work on the human quest for happiness was written by a Holocaust survivor. He doesn't always get credit for it—probably because concentration camps are kind of a bummer—but the Austrian neurologist and psychiatrist Viktor E. Frankl clearly laid the groundwork for contemporary positive psychology with his 1946 book *Man's Search for Meaning*. Frankl wrote, "Everything can be taken from a man but one thing: the last of the human freedoms—to choose one's attitude in any given set of circumstances, to choose one's own way."

The way Frankl saw it, humans discover life's meaning in creative work, in rich and ordinary experiences, in relationships, and in the attitude we choose to take toward unavoidable suffering—in our ability to rejoice even in the midst of hardship. Perhaps life is suffering, but there is light in darkness just as there is tragedy on beautiful blue-sky days.

"I grew up with difficult circumstances—the kind of circumstances that sometimes really break people," Margaret said at our liberation psychology forum. "What happened for me was that I realized at a very young age that my happiness was going to have to come from within. Happiness was somewhere I could go when the scary people weren't around. I wouldn't wish my childhood on anyone, and yet it gave me a resilience."

When I interviewed women about the things that blocked their happiness, I quickly learned that the opposite of joy isn't always depression—it's anxiety. We worry about our health, worry about debt. We worry that we won't live up to our potential, worry that we'll look like fools. We worry about finding a job, worry what will happen if we quit the "good" job we hate. We worry that we'll never find love, worry that we'll lose it. We worry that we're not ready to have kids, worry that we'll get trapped in unwanted family roles, worry that we've waited too long. Anxiety blocks our happiness and inspires us to create even more blocks in our path. We get scared and fidgety, and we start trying to control the people around us. We become overt bullies, or we smile sweet and knife our friends in the back. We smoke a pack a day or eat three meals for breakfast. We create triangles in our relationships by having deceptive affairs. We try to protect ourselves from all these fears by building psychic armor, but we only succeed in warding off potential friendships and rendering ourselves hypersensitive to all life's little annoyances.

As the women on my council of experts kept their journals, happiness often seemed to come as a surprise. "Happiness was so fleeting," Linda wrote. "Like a popping bubble. Brilliant. Like a dream. Five minutes later and it was hard to grasp the thread."

Happiness fluttered in just when we let our guard down and forgot about all the things we were scared of.

The antidotes to fear, then, surely hold some of the secrets to happiness.

What are the antidotes to fear? Meditation, the Buddhists and the scientists tell us. "Mindfulness has been gaining momentum as a healing approach," said Eleanor, a psychologist on my council of experts. "Some therapists have been integrating meditation into their practices—this seems to allow individuals to acknowledge and accept their pain, and be present and more accepting of themselves. I've been meditating and practicing some of these techniques for myself, and they've contributed to a greater sense of peace."

What are the antidotes to fear? Friendship and simple connections. Roslyn's journal entry was typical of the women on my council: "Drinks and talking with J. There's just something to be said for ending the day with someone you love and talking things over. That was the icing on my cake of happiness today."

"It made me happy to decide to make a nice romantic dinner for A.," Sonja wrote. "I cleared the table, had flowers, wine, candle—the house smelling delicious. And we laughed in the middle of the night about a dream."

"K. showed me a piece of art," Calliope wrote. "Talked with M.—she has amazing insights. Laughed on the phone with T. My friends inspire me."

"I felt good talking to S. about child-rearing and being a wife," Eleanor wrote. "Just being able to relate to someone on that level was comforting."

Positive time spent with friends and family relaxes us and predicts our contentment. A 2002 University of Illinois study found that the most salient characteristics shared by students with the highest levels of happiness were their strong ties to friends and family. According to a 2005 *Time* magazine poll, women are even more dependent on social ties.

What are the antidotes to fear? Love, certainly.

M. Scott Peck and bell hooks define love as "the will to extend one's self for the purpose of nurturing one's own or another's spiritual growth." A pretty good working definition, if you ask me. Love is friendship that transcends competition. Love is the kind of marriage that's about nurturing growth rather than about financial or social convenience. Love is maternity. Love is the radical and active choice to care for oneself, for a dog, for a bruised heart, for an old-growth forest.

We care for others, but we also choose to care for ourselves. Through religion, education, and family life, women have been taught the value of selflessness. Feminism blasted through many of the inequities of the past, but a culture doesn't shed hundreds of years of conditioning in the space of a generation or two. Girls are still aware from an early age that we are unworthy or not as worthy, that we can never quite measure up in the eyes of a patriarchal universe. Still, virtually every serious study on happiness points to selflessness—or something akin to it—as a key to lasting contentment. If service is the secret of joy, one has to wonder why waitresses, maids, and mothers aren't the happiest people on earth.

The answer is clear: that service has to be voluntary rather than coerced. And we have to choose, too, to care for ourselves.

Here's where the concept of "metaphysical worthiness" comes in. In Tal Ben-Shahar's slim volume *The Question of Happiness*, he writes, "To lead a happy life we must also experience a sense of metaphysical worthiness. We must appreciate our core self, who we really are, independent of our tangible accomplishments; we must believe that we deserve to be happy; we must feel that we are worthy by virtue of our existence—because we are born with the heart and mind to experience pleasure and meaning."

We deserve to be happy.

"I think there's a cultural understanding that it's selfish to care for ourselves—and this is probably more specific to women—women should be taking care of others, not themselves," Jennifer said at our liberation psychology forum. "Do we deserve to care for ourselves? Do we deserve happiness? I've got to think that women question this more than men."

Calliope agreed. "Women question our right to be happy more than men do, I'm sure of it. And then the question of abuse comes up. When we are abused, we begin to question our self-worth."

In a culture of domination, there is more than enough violence to go around, but there can be little argument that women experience more abuse than men do.

Abuse causes us to dissociate from our bodies, to live in the state of perpetual hypervigilance Barbara Fredrickson warned could cause a downward spiral. Abuse teaches us to mistrust the people who seem to like us, to fall prey to sudden panic or rage. In fear, we rarely get that reprieve from self-consciousness Mihaly Csikszentmihalyi insists we need to experience flow. If the abuse is chronic, we can easily become as helpless as Martin Seligman's dogs, trapped in our shock boxes even after the door has been opened.

What are the antidotes to fear? Some sense of security and freedom from abuse past and present. All times are dangerous times, but we learn to protect ourselves and take care of ourselves to the extent that we can. We learn to relax despite the danger. We learn to recognize when things are not our fault. We don't forget the past, but we learn to see past events in new ways, to move forward with the insight that the past cannot hurt us anymore. We build our self-esteem thusly, sometimes from scratch. We build our sense of metaphysical worthiness.

We learn that we are worthy simply by virtue of our existence.

"All the things that can signify unhappiness—typically, taking things personally, being self-centered, or having unrealistic expectations—all those are connected to thinking that the whole world revolves around me," Jennifer said. "Keeping the journal, I realized that I'm really happy when everyone is really into me, so I have this idea that there's something about people who are able to maintain a bond with the world that is as connected as a mother bond—that they can sustain happiness because they can maintain a sense of security."

We build that sense of security by taking care of ourselves and by opening to the spiritual growth intrinsic in our working definition of love. We build that bond with the world by seeking out connections with people who agree that we are worthy of love and happiness.

What are the antidotes to fear? Resistance and self-determination. We can't avoid all the inequities of life, but we can resist them. We can fight to change them, refuse to be complicit, but refuse, too, to get locked into anger and fear.

Lack of control over negative stimulus was the strongest predictor of depression among Seligman's dogs. But there were exceptions. Some of those dogs—inexplicably—never gave up their quest for freedom.

They never gave up.

"Resistance," Alice Walker has pointed out, "is the secret of joy."

Resistance and self-determination.

"The fact is that human beings come into the world with a passion for control," Daniel Gilbert writes in *Stumbling on Happi-*

ness, "they go out of the world the same way, and research suggests that if they lose their ability to control things at any point between their entrance and their exit, they become unhappy, helpless, hopeless, and depressed." In one study, researchers gave elderly nursing-home residents a houseplant. They told half the residents that they were in control of the plant's care and feeding (high-control group) and told the remaining residents that a staff person would take responsibility for the plant's well-being (low-control group). Six months later, 30 percent of the residents in the low-control group had died, compared with only 15 percent of the residents in the high-control group.

As women, we haven't always been in control of our lives. Sometimes we respond with the neurotic need to control our children, our partners, or our food intake. We choose now to return to a basic sense of control over our own experience. And sometimes we have to begin in small ways.

"It's a positive shift just to learn what an ideal life of one's own would look like," Linda wrote in an e-mail to me after our liberation psychology forum. "To move away from the archetype of the 'hysterical woman' and embrace the value of emotions. Emotions can be a barometer of what needs to change and what's lacking. For instance, if the color of your bathroom upsets you, instead of adapting to it and thinking, 'I always overreact. It's just a color, I must be crazy,' which is the way we have been conditioned, it might be important to change the color. Then there's a relief and then something else might come up, and we can change that, and our pleasure grows and a different kind of awareness can begin to take root. A very simple example, but sometimes things begin on a very basic level."

When we begin to honor our desires on that basic level, we signal our deeper dreams that we're ready for their expression.

In every imperfect day, we make room for the expansive.

listen

❋

I accept an invitation to do a reading at the library on San Juan Island and escape to a tiny cabin without television, computer, or cell phone service. On an early morning hike, I'm startled by rustling branches, a quick wind at the back of my neck. I flinch, look up, and not two-arm's-lengths reach above, a bald eagle takes flight, her wingspan like some giant angel. I stand still and speechless for a long time.

—FROM ARIEL'S JOURNAL

We were taught to ignore our own oppression, smile in false happiness to make our partners comfortable, our children comfortable, our parents comfortable. But oppression is trauma, and trauma can't be forever repressed. We have a right to be angry.

There is power in anger, and we've learned to use that weapon, that tool. We tore down walls.

We ran away, went off to college, moved into the city to find work, to find love. But away from our families and communities we wept, isolated and lonely facing the world as it is. Wide-eyed, we took it all in.

We reached out to elders for hands of support, but they gave us pills that made us weak. Maybe Freud was a misogynist, but at least he sought cures for all that ailed the human psyche. Now our healers doled out symptom relief in fifty-minute hours, billed insurance regardless of whether we were ill or just waking up.

We were told that bliss was ignorant, our happiness uncool. But when we looked around, we noticed that the only ones still laughing were the old radicals, the poets, the mothers who still believed in the world as we could dream it, shooting stars of imagination and ambition—sparks of creativity, of joy.

Proceed from the dream outward, Jung said.

We have the right to make the universe we dream, di Prima said.

The ones who lived in fear and obedience were hardly rewarded for their cool self-protection.

They died with scowls on their faces, heartbroken like the rest of us despite the protection they were promised in exchange for their freedom.

Happiness is a kind of openness, we have learned.

So choose the risky road of power and vulnerability.

Be done with dull things.

Take your life back.

Free yourself from habits of anger and compliance—smoking self-destruction.

Eyes wide open to the world as it is, we grieve.

And in the midst of it all, we rejoice.

Psychological research and our own experience teach us that happiness heals, but the marketing of misery continues, along with quick-fix solutions and endless cultural pressure to be cheerful.

We don't have to accept a psychology that failed us once, failed us twice, failed us three times.

We demand reparations.

We have been told that liberty and happiness are mutually exclusive.

This notion we reject.

We can write our own scripts, write our own stories, take stock of all the things that have made us unhappy. And we can follow the threads of joy, too, like sparks flying from the camp-fire, see where they land.

We can create a liberation psychology.

Every emotion that we feel is real, is the truth.

So we open to love or work or art that feels expansive.

There is no "happily ever after." There is only meditation, action, change, friendship, idea, inspiration, creation.

We spin this light out of darkness.

Happiness is hard work sometimes, but it's good work. It's earthy work. And we are strong and agricultural people. We know how to cultivate a thing or two.

All power to joy, to change, to inspiration, to adaptation, to creation, to remaking the world as we dream it.

sources

※

Alcott, William. *The Young Wife; or, Duties of Woman in the Marriage Relation.* Boston: G. W. Light, 1837.

Allison, Maria, and Margaret Duncan. "Women, Work, and Flow," *Leisure Sciences* 9, no. 3 (1987).

Beauvoir, Simone de. *The Second Sex: The Classic Manifesto of the Liberated Woman.* New York: Vintage Books, 1974.

Beck, Martha. *Finding Your Own North Star: Claiming the Life You Were Meant to Live.* New York: Three Rivers Press, 2001.

Beecher, Catharine, and Harriet Beecher Stowe. *The American Woman's Home; or, Principles of Domestic Science.* New York: J. B. Ford, 1869.

Ben-Shahar, Tal. *The Question of Happiness: On Finding Meaning, Pleasure, and the Ultimate Currency.* San Jose, Calif.: Writers Club Press, 2002.

Bracco, Tara. "Mad Money: Give Bad Situations the Financial Finger with a Fuck You Fund." *Bust Magazine*, March 2008.

Burkeman, Oliver. "How to Be Happy." *Guardian*, May 27, 2006.

Cable, Mary. *American Manners and Morals.* New York: American Heritage, 1969.

Chesler, Phyllis. *Letters to a Young Feminist.* New York: Four Walls Eight Windows, 1998.

———. *Women and Madness: Revised and Updated for the First Time in Thirty Years.* New York: Palgrave Macmillan, 2005.

Chickena, Hib, and Kika Kat. *Off the Map.* Salem, Ore.: Crimeth, 2003.

Clay, Rebecca. "Making Working Families Work," *APA Online* 36, no. 11 (Dec. 2005), www.apa.org/monitor/dec05/work.html.

Csikszentmihalyi, Mihaly. *Flow: The Psychology of Optimal Experience.* New York: Harper Perennial, 1991.

di Prima, Diane. *Recollections of My Life as a Woman: The New York Years.* New York: Penguin, 2001.

———. *Revolutionary Letters.* 5th exp. ed. San Francisco: Last Gasp, 2007.

Ehrenreich, Barbara, and Deirdre English. *For Her Own Good: Two Centuries of Experts' Advice to Women.* New York: Anchor Books, 2005.

Emmons, Robert A. *Thanks! How the New Science of Gratitude Can Make You Happier.* New York: Houghton Mifflin, 2007.

Field, Joanna. *A Life of One's Own.* New York: J. P. Putnam's Sons, 1981.

Frankl, Viktor E. *Man's Search for Meaning.* New York: Beacon Press, 2006.

Fredrickson, Barbara L. "The Broaden-and-Build Theory of Positive Emotions." *Royal Society,* Aug. 17, 2004.

Friedan, Betty. *The Feminine Mystique.* New York: W. W. Norton, 2001.

Geirland, John. "Go with the Flow." *Wired,* Sept. 1996.

Gilbert, Elizabeth. *Eat, Pray, Love.* New York: Penguin, 2006.

Gilligan, Carol. *In a Different Voice.* Cambridge, Mass.: Harvard University Press, 1982.

Gilman, Charlotte Perkins. *"The Yellow Wallpaper" and Other Stories.* Mineola, N.Y.: Dover Publications, 1997.

Guttmacher Institute, www.guttmacher.org.

Haidt, Jonathan. *The Happiness Hypothesis: Finding Modern Truth in Ancient Wisdom.* New York: Basic Books, 2006.

Healy, David. *The Antidepressant Era.* Cambridge, Mass.: Harvard University Press, 1997.

Hochschild, Arlie Russell. *The Managed Heart: Commercialization of Human Feeling.* Berkeley: University of California Press, 2003.

Jack, Dana Crowley. *Silencing the Self: Women and Depression.* New York: Harper Perennial, 1991.

Johnson, George. "Favored by the Gods." *Scientific American,* May 22, 2006.

Kotchemidova, Christina. "From Good Cheer to 'Drive-By Smiling': A Social History of Cheerfulness," *Journal of Social History* 39, no. 1 (Fall 2005).

Lucas, Richard E. "Adaptation and the Set-Point Model of Subjective Well-Being: Does Happiness Change After Major Life Events?" *Current Directions in Psychological Science* 16, no. 2 (2007).

Maddux, James E. "Stopping the 'Madness': Positive Psychology and the Deconstruction of the Illness Ideology and the *DSM.*" In *Handbook of Positive Psychology,* edited by C. R. Snyder and Shane J. Lopez. New York: Oxford University Press, 2002.

Maines, Rachel. *The Technology of Orgasm: "Hysteria," the Vibrator, and Women's Sexual Satisfaction.* Baltimore: Johns Hopkins University Press, 1999.

Martens, China. *The Future Generation: The Zine-Book for Subculture Parents, Kids, Friends & Others.* Baltimore: Atomic Book Company, 2007.

Miller, Jacquelyn C. "An 'Uncommon Tranquility of Mind': Emotional Self-Control and the Construction of a Middle-Class Identity in Eighteenth-Century Philadelphia," *Journal of Social History* 30, no. 1 (1996).

The Old Farmer's Almanac, www.almanac.com/weatherhistory.

Psychiatry Online, www.psychservices.psychiatryonline.org/cgi/issue_pdf/backmatter_pdf/9/1.pdf.

Saint-Exupéry, Antoine de. *The Little Prince.* Translated by Katherine Woods. New York: Harcourt, Brace & World, 1943.

Salzberg, Sharon. *Lovingkindness: The Revolutionary Art of Happiness.* Boston: Shambhala, 1997.

Seligman, Martin. *Authentic Happiness: Using the New Positive Psychology to Realize Your Potential for Lasting Fulfillment.* New York: Free Press, 2002.

Senior, Jennifer. "Some Dark Thoughts on Happiness," *New York,* July 10, 2006.

Smith, Johni. *How to Be a Flight Stewardess or Steward: A Handbook and Training Manual for Airline Cabin Attendants.* North Hollywood, Calif.: Pan American Navigation Service, 1974.

Thakor, Manisha, and Sharon Kedar. *On My Own Two Feet: A Modern Girl's Guide to Personal Finance.* Minneapolis: Adams Business, 2007.

Thomas, Marlo. "Housework." Performed by Carol Channing. *Free to Be . . . You and Me.* Arista Records, 1972.

University of Iowa News Service, "Low Income Women More Likely to Suffer from Postpartum Depression," Feb. 19, 2008.

USA Today, "Depression Among College Students Rising," May 21, 2003.

U.S. Census Bureau, www.census.gov.

Yunus, Muhammad. *Creating a World Without Poverty: Social Business and the Future of Capitalism.* New York: PublicAffairs, 2007.

acknowledgments

※

I owe handwritten thank-you notes to my editors, Denise Oswald and Gena Hamshaw, and to my agent, Faye Bender—three amazing women who, through all the life chaos of baby-making, publishing-world drama, and extremely awkward yoga poses, proved to me that yes, it is possible to be smart and empowered *and* to prioritize happiness.

Imagine added hand-screened prints to those handwritten notes. I owe much art and love to the hundreds of women who participated in the research I report. Thanks to all who shared their lives and thoughts with me by answering my endless surveys and questions, and thanks to the smaller group, my council of experts—your generosity, spirit, and intelligence are inspiring. Thanks also to the lovely Dexter Flowers, who served as our council's scribe.

Bluebird is a better book thanks to Margaret McConnell, Moe Bowstern, and Maria Fabulosa, who read and critiqued drafts.

As life would have it, one of the practices that has stuck with me after all the pursuit chronicled in these pages is one I didn't write much about. So it's an addendum—a shout-out to the ladies of the Bhaktishop yoga studio in Portland. As much as my angst-ridden philosophical background wishes it weren't true, well, it's true—just go do some yoga. It's cheaper than Prozac. And it makes you strong.

Pure gratitude, finally and always, to Maia and Maximilian. May you be free. And may you be happy.